ORPHANED LATITUDES

Gérard Rudolf

To Janet,

Thank you for listening.

Kind regards,

Gérard Rudolf

Red Squirrel Press

ISBN: 978-1-906700-18-8

First published in the UK in 2009
by Red Squirrel Press
PO Box 219 Morpeth NE61 9AU
www.redsquirrelpress.com

Typeset in Georgia

Printed by Athenaeum Press Ltd,
Gateshead. Tyne & Wear

Cover Design: Pluto Panoussis – www.pickle@mweb.co.za

Acknowledgements

My love and deepest gratitude to Hermarette for giving me the courage to want something ... and for the roof over my head.

J. H. - *true friendships are hard to explain.*

Special thanks to the *Bird Head Son* who told me about: *"...the muscle in the air..."*

Thanks due: Sheila Wakefield, Josephine Scott, the High Level Bridge Poets for giving me a place at the table, for their encouragement and the intense Saturday afternoons spent in their company at the Bridge Hotel. Ditto the members of the Salsa Club Writers. Also Fredrik Elg who translated some of my work into Swedish, Peter Kayode Adegbie, Charles Gardiner, Jeff Price, Sheree Mack, Angela Readman, Stevie Ronnie, Elizabeth Whyman, Toast Coetzer and Jaco Botha.

Last Days of the Comeback Kid won first prize in the 2008 CRUSE Poetry Competition and appears in the resulting anthology, Rowing Home. *Last Reel (American Ending)* and *You are Here, 1957- 1993* appeared on the ID on Tyne website as poems of the week. Insolent Rudder published *Smoking a Joint with a Stone Age Man.* Ons Kleintji magazine, Cape Town, published early drafts of *Stones, Last Days of the Comeback Kid, Shelling Peanuts, Christ Re-Entering Cape Town* and *Darth Vader, John the Baptist and a Dead Fish. A Sixteen Line Portrait of Fredrik in his Garden (Behind His Red House)* appeared in the 2006 anthology, Identity, published as part of the Newcastle Lit & Phil Poetry Day programme. *Circa* appears in the 2007 anthology Sepia Souls also by ID on Tyne. The latter along with *14th Avenue, Tshwane (née Pretoria), Overnight Commercial Flight, Dig for New Shoes, Christ Re-entering Cape Town,* and *Two Towns* were published in the anthology, Streams of the Soul, edited by Jack Mapanje and Peter Kayode Adegbie. *Bunches of Bananas Wrapped in Boxing Gloves* appeared in the American journal, Night Train. *Emily Melting* appears in The Book of Ten, Zebra Publishing, 2009.

#152 Gérard Rudolf

Gérard Rudolf was born in Pretoria, South Africa. He spent most of his childhood in Cape Town. When he was a kid, he was utterly convinced the world had been monochrome before he was born—all the photographs in the family albums, the old movies on TV, all of it black and white. He spent hours trying to figure out how and when the world changed to colour. He roamed the neighborhood with friends creating strange worlds in empty lots—Cowboys and Indians, Star Wars, also some Huck Finn. He studied the usual subjects, but school bored him. He stared out the windows. His head was never where his body was. It still isn't. His teenage years were spent in Johannesburg. He played rugby to please his father, but never had any great interest in sports apart from swimming. At 15 he faked a neck injury to get out of playing rugby and that might be considered the beginning of his acting career. After school, he joined the military for 2 years because it was compulsory. His family didn't have enough money to send him into exile in order to dodge the draft. At 18 he did a tour of duty in the Angolan War. After his discharge he resolved never to wear a uniform or take up arms again. He studied acting and became a successful actor. He loved the collaborative nature of acting, all the oddballs and geniuses, and that no two days were the same. In 1993 his older brother, an archeologist, died in a car accident and that shocked him into the realization that we only have right now. In 1998 he co-founded a professional acting school in Cape Town because he wanted to give something back to the industry that had saved him from the 9-5. But in 2002 he found himself burnt out. He thought Cape Town had fallen out of love with him. His life was burning down around his ears. He felt as if he were sitting in a deck chair with a cold beer watching everything go up in smoke. He quit acting, got divorced, and moved to the UK two days later where he started writing full-time to orient himself on the map. In 2006, his father died and he became even more aware of his mortality. He is not as dark and moody as people think. He blames this misconception on his face.

For my father who tried to look to the future.

For my brother who dug up the past.

CONTENTS

CONTENTS

Rough Blues for a Chev Impala
Friends of Jesus
Taste of Thoughts
A Sixteen Line Portrait of Fredrik in His Garden (Behind His Red House)
Seven for a Missing Friend
1. Johnny Depp's Mouth
2. International Bastard
3. Puke and Love in the Bathhouse
4. Personal Hygiene Department
5. Maxim
6. 20/20 Vision
7. "...the summer that men first walked on the moon."

End Credits

"...This is what
you want to remember, the map
you will follow: how it is
to be admired; to be good
as any man."

*The Toast of the Kit-Cat Cl*ub, Linda France

First Dispatch

Date: Wed, 17 Mar 2005 02:51:19 +0000 (GMT)
From: "Gerard Rudolf" <gerardrudolf@yahoo.co.uk>
Subject: Sleep facing South
To: "G.W." <*********@*********.com>

It's 1:57am here. (3:57 there. Christ...) 'can't sleep, don't want to sleep, need sleep, won't sleep...

I really don't know what it is I want to say. Just talk.

There's a park right opposite my flat. When the world calms down round about now I can hear birds singing and chirping in the trees. It is the strangest thing. I have no idea what kinds of birds are wide-awake this time of the night. I usually listen to them chittering away while I drift off to sleep.

The birds remind me of my late teens. My best friend and I used to go clubbing in central Joburg back when it was still reasonably OK to be out on the streets of the city at 5 am. (And you know what Joburg is like these days, right?) We used to frequent a club called DV8 just off Joubert Park. We were under aged but somehow always managed to blag our way into the dingy place to see some of our favourite bands: Asylum Kids, The Sons of Gaddafi Bar Mitzvah Band, Dog Detachment, The Cherryfaced Lurchers (fronted by a very young James Phillips or *Bernoldus Niemand* as he was then known)... I'm sure you can recall some of them. They railed against the Nationalist Government, Conscription, the World In General. They meant nothing to the world beyond Joburg, to the world beyond our dark borders. But they meant the world to us. They kept us sane. They kept us angry.

Anyway, we'd usually stagger out of there around 3 or 4 am on a school night, slightly pissed and reeking of cigarettes and Redheart Rum 'n Coke (the cheapest booze we could get), and we'd start the long walk back to our world, back to soft, safe, leafy, white middle class suburbia, a walk of about 2 hours or so. On the way we passed the graffiti painted on those red brick inner city walls: "FREE MANDELA!!!" or "HANG MANDELA", "ONE MAN ONE VOTE", "VIVA ANC", "ONE SETTLER, ONE BULLET", ... all in huge, crude dripping white or yellow letters. We hardly understood who this Mandela was. To us he was just a name painted on walls by angry black people. At the time the regime's propaganda sold him as a terrorist from a time before we were born, a dangerous Commie ghost, hater of white people and the government's most feared bogey-man-terrorist. We were boys but we sensed our leaders in their cheap three-piece suits and ridiculous trilbies were not to be trusted. We heard rumours of sinister government hit squads embarking on "cross-border raids" killing or capturing "terrorists" and detaining them without trial and murdering militant political figures like Steve Biko, the Guguletho Seven and many more. There were raids on the homes of white academics, writers and journalists. (How long did Breyten Breytenbach and many others rot in solitary confinement? What about Neil Aggett who "slipped on a piece of soap"? In the end, what was it all for?) We watched news footage of riots on university campuses - German Shepherds drawing blood from the heels of fleeing students, the torn banners, truncheons crushing skulls and ribs, the clouds of tear gas, rocks raining down like a biblical plague. Sometimes we could smell the townships outside the city burning when the wind blew in the right/wrong? direction. We were convinced the country would be razed in front of our eyes, that we would definitely pay for the sins of our fathers, see their monuments and institutions trampled to dust and that we'd be chased into the same icy ocean from which our stinking, scurvy-riddled forefathers had crawled. We all sensed the end of our fathers' age approaching years, decades before it happened. We could fucking taste the bitter fruit, smell the rot at the roots. Wonders and clemency never had an easy ride in Africa. We expected no miracles, no mercy. Africa was bearing down on us like a killer in the night. Remember? Do you remember how nobody around us said anything about these things out loud?

As we walked home we heard birds waking up all over the deserted predawn city. (Always a depressing time of the day for me) We talked about the gig or some sexy chick back at the club or just mused about the future - our immediate futures holding nothing for us but 2 years in the SADF. And this is what the birds here remind me of tonight: us, me back in the gloom that was '82 Joburg - clueless, choiceless, a virgin and petrified I'd die a virgin in some forsaken, fly infested corner of Angola. We were so unaware of how big and sinister this world really is and that in some cities, far away from that godless place of blood, flames, fear, lies, death, paranoia and disinformation, some birds never go to sleep.

On nights like tonight a tenacious wind winnows through the bony branches of the trees in the park. It sounds like the incoming tide off Sea Point on a summer's evening or the Black South Easter, the Cape Doctor, blasting off the back of Devil's Peak and howling down the slopes of the mountain straight through the guava tree in my old back yard in James Street as it chases dry leaves around the corners of the house. It is not a happy sound. It is not a sad sound either. It's a sound inside me, a sound I have carried with me for the longest time. It is a sonic link, an invisible cord/chord that stretches from the heart of that country all the way to the neglected latitudes of my own heart. Now, here, inside that forlorn wail outside the window I hear, no, 'see' a dry season, smell the wild odour of fynbos* and pine on the slopes of Table Mountain as the city cools in the small-hour darkness after a blistering white day.

Tonight I'll leave my window cracked open, just wide enough for my history to waft through, for it to get snagged in the yellow curtain like shimmering sardines in a net. I'll keep an ear out for messages from the streets I know like I know my own pitted face. I'll listen for bulletins from all the trees I climbed as a boy, from aloes that pricked me, from all the creaking houses I've ever slept in. I'll listen for voices from my past disguised as bird song hidden under the white noise of the wind and wait for them to tell me everything will be OK again...some day.

It is 4:45 back home now, only 2:45 here.

I'm done talking.

I hope you are well. I really do.

Love to A. Love to everybody down there in the Deep South. I miss you. I miss the heat at this time of year as summer gears up for her grand exit. I miss the dawn chorus of African birds.

But not enough to be there.

GR

PS: I guess I should brush up on my ornithological knowledge and find out about the strange night birds that keep me awake. (Blackbirds?) I should learn the names of the trees in the park opposite the flat and begin to map the lay of this new land.

        Not tonight. Enough is enough.

Tonight I'll hang a hammock between time zones. Sleep with my head facing south.

---

* **Fynbos**: meaning "fine bush" in Afrikaans. Natural shrub land vegetation occurring in a small belt of the Western Cape, South Africa.

...the summer that men first walked on the moon.

Il me semble que je serais toujours bien là où je ne suis pas.

Baudelaire

A Short History of Aloes: He is still there, square inside that old afternoon, holding an air rifle. He shoots a hole in a fat aloe leaf. Sap bleeds from the hole. The sap is thick; the texture of golden syrup, cough mixture. He pokes his index finger in the sap. He holds the smear of aloe sap on his fingertip close to my lips and orders me to close my eyes and to stick out my tongue. I trust him. I trust him because he is my brother. I do as he says. He drags his sap-smeared fingertip carefully over my tongue, orders me to close my mouth, to swallow. The sap is bitter - more bitter than anything I have ever had to swallow before. I gag, collapse onto my hands and knees like a dog. I puke until every muscle in my small body aches. I puke until it feels as if my ribs might rip through the skin, until there is nothing left to puke. My brother laughs. I am four years old. He is thirteen.
I trust him until he dies twenty-three years later in the heart of the country.

In the veld near the mangled wreck,
a patch of aloes in bloom -
their flowers: yellow brushes dipped in red paint.
Their bitter lessons wait
patiently for unsuspecting tongues.

CIRCA

- a composition for voices -

this is the Stone Age.
this is the first page.
days are dateless, endless, and things await their names.
this is where i start.
this is the place, this is my heart.

Two things:

1.   **A telephone**: too big for my hand, its mouthpiece shaped like a shell. It is unpredictable, makes me jump when it trrings like a bell. It is a bakelite thing but I don't know bakelite yet. It's an instrument wired with mysteries in a time of five digit numbers inside thin directories.

2.   **A footprint**: in cement placed there with my father's help. This is the first firm record of my existence. My footprint says:

> here he is,
> scarce three years off his hands and knees,
> vertical, shy,
> a sprig searching out the sky.
> ↑
> ### ← *this is where The World begins (and ends)* →
> ↓

The Four Fences of The World and a Secret Hole: The World is a small house in a suburb. The house is solid, made of red brick, sober red roof, maybe half an acre of land. I don't know what suburb is, or red or acre.   **1.**   One side of The World is fenced with black split poles that reach to stars, when it rains it gives off the smell of tar.   **2.**   The opposite side of The World is marked by a row of soaring quince trees - although I do not know they are quince trees yet.

> odd yellow fruit plucked and sliced by my mother's hand.
> it robs my mouth of spit.
> the flesh contains fine grit.
> are these things made of sand?

The quince trees stand not far from my bedroom window. I listen wide-eyed as they snag the wind at night, tortures it until it falls to the ground where it dies without a sound. In the morning I look for the wind among twigs and brown leaves, find nothing but the sour rot of fruit, the silver criss-cross slithers of snails. I learn to believe in invisible things.   **3.**   The back edge of The World is also a thicket of trees. These trees are so dense, so dark, so tall I think it really is the edge of The World. Somewhere behind them dogs bark and growl and cats yowl like my baby sister. Sometimes girls scream.   **4.**   This border is also dark but different:

> it is flat and black and solid,
> a white line runs down the middle of it.

I am banned from crossing its span alone. When I think nobody is looking, I stand on its edge, gouge clots from the red soil and lob them across it just to see what would happen. From here I can see more houses. They are different from the one I live in. I learn my World is not the only World. I begin to suspect there are many Worlds all around. I hear them when I put my ear to a crack in the split pole fence. When I push leaves and branches out of the way with my hands I see them with my own eyes. Sometimes I see other people too. Some of them are my size.

> others are taller than my father and mother,
> some are somewhere in between just like my brother.
> some wave at me and i wave back.
> i want to reach them. i want to cross the river of black.

14

I attempt it several times only to be plucked back violently by my mother or my brother. These Other Worlds become my first fear, my first challenge, my first obsession. Later I discover a boy-sized hole in the quince tree fence. I snake through and emerge head first somewhere else with warm scratches on my arms and legs. I think I am alone for the first time, alone inside another World. But there is a boy just like me. We stare at each other.

our shadows are long and black.
something makes a fist inside my stomach.
he speaks his name.
i speak mine.
we are eye-to-eye.
his hair's aflame.

He shows me an old mulberry tree at the heart of his World. I don't know it's a mulberry tree, I don't know it is old. The tree is tall and it tells me I am small. He shows me how to climb the tree and eat its black fruit. The fruit is sweet and wild and we laugh at each other through bruised lips, lick sticky fingers with purple tongues. We are hairless apes without tails. We ingest The World around us, compete with birds and worms and ants, invent words for things below/above/outside us. We become The World we're in.

```
sun/moon
            cloud
                  bird              ?  ?
                                    ↑  ↑
                          (end of) The World
        him/them                    x
X - mulberry tree               (my footprint)
? ←    The World ¦ quince tree fence   HOME    split poles ¦ The World →
            Dad+ Mom - brother >me< sister + Emily
                                        bee
            grass                    flower
                                          ant
                                    stone/sand
                  !street!
                     ?
←_____→

                     ?
                     ↑
            ? ← World → ?
                     ↓
                     ?
```

so things become words and words become things.
so they will remain and so the world begins.
we misplaced days inside that tree,
or so it seemed to me.

It becomes easier to move to-and-fro between the Worlds through the hole in the quince tree fence. I depart clean, return with pockets full of new words and black fingers and dark stains on my legs and shirt when I hear my mother's call. I learn some stains only fade with time, some not at all. Sometimes my shit is purple and my brother laughs as my mother wipes my arse.

Brother, where are you now?

•

night outside, familiar people around a large table.
food. the clicketyclack of a family meal. talk. The World feels stable.

At the table I learn what my mouth likes and my nose tells me what my stomach will always reject. It is a time of trial and error. Over days like years, fast lessons arrive with bleeding knees, bumps on the head and with devil thorns in my bare feet. There are other nights with all of us together around a huge radiogram. Underneath it on the carpet staring into its dark universe is where I am. I see a tiny light among wires and dust: God's crimson eye looking down on us. There are people inside the machine. I can hear their voices but they are hidden deep.

(peep...peep... peep... peep... Dit is Radio Suid Afrika...)

i listen to God's Voice as i fall asleep, asleep, asleep,
dream of a hole in a fence...

•

Yes, she too is always here:

Emily:
big and black as the African night.
her smile is broad and ultra white.
her eyes are brown and full of hope.
she smells of snuff and Sunlight soap.

She lives in the outbuilding where my footprint is. There are many others like her in The World. They look different from me, from us, although we share the same World. When they're together they sing in a beautiful language we can't understand. My father says she is *Zu-lu.* Inside her room in the middle of the day she feeds me corn meal porridge crumbly as clay with sour milk and butter and loads of sugar. The porridge makes bones strong and muscles big so I can one day slay a lion like the one on the syrup tin – or so she says. Her bed stands on bricks. Why? I ask. Because of *Tokoloshe,* she says.

the bed is tall because *Tokoloshe* is small.
he has only one leg, he comes in on moonless nights,
he steals women and calls out men to brawl.
Tokoloshe eats children when they switch off the lights.
he roams the earth on a hyena's bare back
and keeps a knife in an old zebra skin sack.
he's a devil, a *tsotsi*[†], he has no fears.
(my eyes are big, i'm fighting off tears.)
thula, thula, she whispers, and drips more Africa into my ears.

And where is Emily now?

•

Epilogue: Blanket in hand and silent, staring at my father's back as he stands on a dark *stoep* smoking a cigarette, burning star-sized holes in the African night. He turns around, sees me, picks me up, and we sit together in silence in a creaking chair. His silence smells like tobacco smoke. We sit like this until my body goes limp. But there is something else; a whiff, a new aroma hitching an easy ride on the back of a cricket's pulse. I ask what the smell is and my father slowly sounds the word that will stay married to the thing:

fran-gi-pa-ni

the word is the smell of my father under the skin of Home.
it is my favourite smell, my favourite word.

And where is my father now?

[†] gangster

16

•

to this i shall return,
to Adam before The Fall,
where frangipani flowers burn,
where, at last, i'll know not I at all.
i must be close to Home.
look, my footprint –
ancient, fossilised, stone.
all these things and all these things.
and somewhere a telephone rings and ringsandringsringsringsringsringsringsrings...

Two Studies in Defective Recall

1.

Day:

      Bug-eyed boy inside a department store. Everything looks new, unused, unblemished, full of potential, the way things used to look in the late sixties. The boy is doing his best to keep up with his mother's stride. He's transfixed by his mother's upside-down reflection rippling underneath the surface of a polished floor. He is looking down into the Other World, down onto the ceiling with its white sheen and broken lines of glowing strip lights - perforations in a giant sheet of paper.

      The clickclackclickclackclick of his mother's heels on gleaming melamine.

Later:

      On sandaled toes mesmerised by a wind-up toy on a table: a fat tin man frantically beating a bass drum. The drum seems to bloat from his belly like a moon. The white tabletop is crowded with many different wind-up toys. They are all moving and crashing into each other: on a tricycle a monkey with a propeller-topped fez goes round in circles, two shiny lumberjacks try to saw a log in half, a robot with flickering blue lights for eyes sputters sparks from its claws, a boxer takes swipes at nothing and a smiling man in a small row boat heads for the edge of the world. It is the fat man with the shiny key buried between his shoulder blades, the one beating the big round drum that holds the boy's gaze. Mysterious cogs and gears move in the darkness beneath his metal skin. The boy strains to get at him.

      Sweaty fingers splayed open at the end of an arm.

Later:

      He surfaces from the depths of sleep. He is no longer inside his own home, his own room, his own bed, but there are no questions of alarm. He knows exactly where he is. He also knows he is not awake. He knows he is inside the fat drummer's drum. He knows because he can see soft morning light seeping through the drum's vellum walls. He sees himself curled up in the curve of the giant drum. He is clutching a blanket.

      He wants to stay there looking at himself sleeping in the white light.

2.

Navy Blue Suit with Short Trousers: and long black socks up to the knees. Black lace-up shoes. The boy is slightly older. It is mid summer and the days have names: This day is Sunday. It is Sunday because no other day feels like Sunday. Sundays are long and quiet and boring even before Sunday starts. Sundays smell of burning fat and barbeque fires. On Sundays the entire world is trapped in stasis. The boy in the navy blue suit is walking on a cement pavement. He is thinking his own thoughts as he walks. He is flying over a flat landscape. The cracks in the pavement are tree-lined rivers down below. The Sunday sun stings the back of his head. It feels pleasant. There is a man-boy walking beside him. The man-boy is holding his hand. His hand is smaller than the man-boy's hand. He feels safe, protected by the contact of hands. The other hand is familiar. He knows it is his brother's hand. His brother is tall and real, more real than the world the boy occupies. The feeling of hands touching is a reminder that there is still another world beyond his world of flat grey landscapes inhabited by curious creatures with many legs and no voices. He feels as if he is dangling from his brother's hand, floating inside a bubble.

      He is confident he'll be plucked out whenever he wishes.

      Now they are standing still. He is looking down into the water of a small brook; head pushed through the scuffed railing of the bridge. The water is perfectly still as if it had stopped flowing under the weight of the day. There are white clouds and a blue sky at the bottom of the brook. Perhaps it is not a brook at all but a sliver of sky that somebody had torn off and left right there in the middle of the open field. He hears a voice from far away, sees a hand, a finger pointing down at the slither of sky. He looks at the hand and follows the pointing finger downwards... What? What *is* there under the surface? His eyes quickly learn to find the bends in the light, to look beyond the clouds, through the sky, to see inside the water. There, behind the glimmer, a fish floating almost motionless just below the surface.

The fish is too big for the pool it's in.

The boy is fascinated, frightened by the curious fish that fell to earth with the sky. He can feel claustrophobia fidgeting like ants deep inside the creature's brain. The eyes show no emotion, no signs of panic. No cry for help bubbles from its toothless yawn. It is simply waiting, praying to its god for the day to pass, for the sky to fall back into place again. Sunlight ignites its scales. They flash like knives in a cave. Is the fish made of metal just like the fat drummer who now lives on the floor under the boy's bed? He becomes aware of his hand sweating inside his brother's hand. Cold sweat pearls on his skin below the dark confines of his suit. He looks up. The sun blinds him.

His brother is a black shape.

That night, tucked up in his bed, the boy can still feel the fish inside his brain. He tries to imagine what it would feel like to float up there in the blue sky, far above the heat and cracked pavements and the lead of Sunday.

Float with clouds and strange fish.

19

Blown Away

The wind ransacks a black shore for the remains of a summer,
finds only a billowing shirt, the bare feet of a boy -
sunburnt toes feel for cracks or any hold
they can find on the surface of cold clints.

But the boy is held fast by darkness gathering far offshore.
He imagines he sees the approach of the end of time -
far more fascinating than the unfinished lessons
from History, the sober rules
of Math abandoned in his room.

'Wind', the boy prays,
'rip this shirt off my
back. Hack the hide from my
flesh. Whittle the flesh from my
bones. Shake the fear from my head,

'and, decades later, blow me back
to those who never gave up waiting for me.
I'll join them again at the round table deep inside
the hub of a suburban home – a boy no more –
and they will not recognise me as their own.'

Can wind do such a thing
to a boy? Blow him away
for decades, or just
for one day?

Emily: (a slight return) Three Monsters of the African Night

1.

Bed on Bricks and a Cricket Bat: She smelled of snuff and Sunlight Soap. She wore a headscarf. She was big and black. She took her time walking from here to there as if time was hers to take. She had her own room in our backyard. I used to visit her in her room. She had placed three bricks under each leg of her bed. One day I asked her about her bed on bricks. She told me the bricks are protection against *Tokoloshe*, a short one-legged imp. He murders women on full-moon nights. *Tokoloshe* fights men and if a man wins the fight *Tokoloshe* will bless him with powers of healing. She said the bricks give the bed height to prevent *Tokoloshe* from reaching her while she sleeps.

For years I checked the phases of the moon every night, pondered the height of my own bed. On full moon nights I cradled my brother's cricket bat under the sheets.

This was thirty-eight years ago. I can still smell the lacquered willow, the wild sourness of the sweat-stained grip.

2. Teeth of a Baboon

She told me the story of *Antjie Somers* who catches naughty children and eats them. A man in women's clothes, teeth of a baboon, he carries a rusty knife under his dress, breaks into houses, kills the children before riding off into the night on the back of a huge hyena, the severed ears and noses of dead children on a string around his neck. Emily knew the names of all the monsters in the African night.

I never visited her in her room after sunset again. The path to Emily's room was too dark for a boy with an imagination.

3.
Emily Melting

me through the back window of the car
just looking at her
her rich soil & soap smell still on my shirt

       finally

this is poor memory ~

i am alone in that car
a boy   five
driving itself down that street
for the final time

       no steadfast father behind the black wheel
       no mother with hands sewn together in her lap like nothing they can do
       no brother who points at things and says
i spy...
       no crying babe-in-arms sister
       no sun-ripened loquats on the trees to tempt me
       with their yellow voices

&

       no radio providing an exit song

no

just me watching her melt
under the sun
      into soil
      into the scratchy day   Vanishing

arm hovering in the   air   as if she thought of a solution...
hand over mouth

choking an objection?

me & her   Emily
melting into the country that made us both
made us all

melt

that was 1971

All Points South

You are Here, 1957 - 1993

(Inspired by *KAROO MOONS*, Richard Mark Dobson & Ruben Mowszowski. STRUIK, 2004)

Still dark.
You are in a car.
Black road ahead.
Poles bend past the side window.
Bushes blur. *Koppies* drift. Far off mountains move slower.
The smell of drought.
You are driving through sameness. The sameness of life.
You speed up. Hot tyres drone on cold tar.
Below the tar, a forgotten dirt track.
Deeper still insects tunnel. Roots. Eyeless things.
Now, dig deeper.
Crystalline forms. Fractals.
Below that shells and bones of ancient fish.
Petrified ocean old as stars.
Walls between mind and matter melt. Glacier slow.

You are here.
You live here.
You have always been here.
Terrene, clotted with rootedness.

You are stone. Sand. Dust. Powder. Particle.
The past is the present. The past brought you here.
Time is the endless fence rushing past.
Yet there are other parts to the moment.
The moment is connected to the fading stars.
Solar winds billow beyond imagination. Air in your nostrils.
Air made by plants.
Time here is time termless. Earth and sky.
Dig here and you emerge among the stars.
Die here and you'll be back in the cradle.
Life here begins where astronomers' laws never existed.
Then the sun.
It flares over the far horizon.
Swallow scuds from a thorny bush.
First light.

Second Dispatch (Translated from Afrikaans)

Sun Mountain, 7
Mark Ave.
North Cliff
Johannesburg
2195

2 August 1984
Howzit Ma and Pa!
I am sitting in the ███ ████ typing this because you know what
my handriting look like!
We are here now. its a ugly place. you know how I hate dry and hot
places. Tolerating it. Smells of dust and fire.
Anyway we only left ████████ at around ██████████. ███
flight. I am not very sure where I am. All I know is it is in ██
██ near the ██████ The base is not too bad. It is well laid out.
Swimming pool. Bar. A canteen with a snooker table, a TV and a video
machine for saturda night movies and we get tapes of the Currie Cup
games but a month later. There is also a small shop that isopen on
weekends where we can buy cigarettes, chips chocolates, cokes and
fanta orange, soap and so on. We sleep in ██████████. ██
███████████ but they are very comfortable and best of all very
cool during the day. All the showers are outside under some thorn
trees. Not too bad. We eve have a coffee bar for the troops where we
can buy toasted sarmies (25c), donuts (10c) and coffee, tea(15c). But
most of us go for the bar at the end of the day. (███ is cheaper
than coke! Sorry Ma)Its called the Utopia House.
It is HOT. 35 degrees during the day!!!
The base is right on the ██████████ and we can see a ████████
████ from here. If look through the binocs you can see their guys
walking around and doing things. Weird. They watch us too probably.
But I cant say too much because they might sensor my entire letter
and all youl'l get in the mail is a black sheet of paper! Not so
nice. We are not even allowed to take photographs of anything.
There is a lot of wild life here. Last night while I ████████
████ an elephant walked right by █ ████████. It was so close to me I
could have reached out and touched it. and baboons everywhere. There
are fish eagles around the river. They are so beautiful. At night you
can hear the hippos crashing through the reeds on the ██████████
side. They tell us hippos are dangerous and to stay out of their way.
Then there is the usual scorpions, snakes and spiders. We find little
scorpions on our mosquito nets in the morning. Millions of mosquitoes
at night. During the day mompanie flies get in our ears and noses and
mouths. This place is like real Africa. I dont think the people want
us here. We dont want to really be here. Not much choice for us.
Nothing has happened yet. We ll be going for our first long patrol in
██. The guys dont talk about this
much. Most of us just want to get through this alive and back to the
States I think. I know I do. You know I am not really the outdoors
type hey. But it is not too bad here and you dont have to worry about
me. But you probably will. War is just hurry up and wait. Dad, give
mom and Liesel a hug and kiss from me. Enjoy the rugby and the golf,
dad. Do not work so hard.I hope the Blue Bulls win the cup. Ma, send
some biltong or canned peaches. please. And tell Pieter thanks for
the books. I will see you in ██████████ Not long hey. home is far
from here. I miss you.
Love.G. xxx PS: Tell Liesel to stay out of my room. she can play my
records if she wants but she musnt scratch them. NOt the Bob Marley
or springsteen ones.

Fear and Cordite

1.

Shelling Peanuts: Early afternoon. I am walking through a smouldering war-torn village of mud- and straw huts. Rotting livestock broil in the midday sun. The stench is unbelievable. All sound disturbed by silence. I nearly trip over an old Ovambo woman sitting contentedly in the shade of her ruined hut. She is shelling peanuts into a wooden bowl. She seems oblivious of me. It is as if she's asleep in the world and I am her dream. She is humming a tune. The tune is devoid of melody, abstract, a thought without root. Her legs are stretched out in front of her. Her feet are covered in pale dust. The soles of her feet are hard and thick from a lifetime of walking on hot sand. Long, spindly fingers. The knuckles are knots in elephant grass. Her dress is filthy, decaying. One breast is showing; a sundried fig. Her left eye is bruised and swollen shut, bottom lip split open. The scab is swarming with tiny *mompanie* flies. She makes no effort to shoo the flies away. I offer her water from my canteen, an army-issue energy bar. It is all I have. She doesn't look up from her task. Her life is shelling peanuts into that wooden bowl. I wonder what I would do if she was my mother. I wonder if she'll ever need anything again. I snap a picture of her and run to catch up with my platoon. I still have her image somewhere. I usually stumble across her when I'm looking for something else.

2.

Afrika's Not for Sissies: That same afternoon I have a conversation with a soldier from another unit. He is a professional soldier, an Ovambo. He grew up in a tiny village nearby. His entire family was wiped out by SWAPO soldiers when he was twelve. He ran away and hid in a crocodile infested river for three days. He survived on frogs and plants.
He says he entered that river a boy, emerged from the reeds and mud a man.
He says the only way he wants to die is with an AK47 bullet right between the eyes.
He grins at the shocked expression on my face.
He says: Afrika's not for sissies, bru. Neither is this life.
Nothing about Africa ever shocks me again.

3.

Smoking a Joint with a Stone Age Man: That night I am supposed to be on guard duty. Instead I am sharing a small fire with a Bushman tracker. He's a member of my platoon. I watch him roll a Cuban cigar-sized joint with a page from a battered Gideon's Bible. We smoke in silence, pass it to-and-fro between us like ideas in a conversation. Dagga seeds pop and crackle. He folds the night, the fire, us, inside a song about the Moon and the Holy Mantis. It is a hymn in a prehistoric tongue of insect clicks and meandering hums. His language is old as stone. His language is the First Language, a language borrowed from plants and animals and insects, plucked from the ether at the dawn of history. It is The Mother Tongue. I want to cry because I am stoned, because of the way his tiny frame seems to drown inside his brown combat uniform, because I know he'd rather carry a bow and a quiver of poisoned arrows than an R-4 assault rifle. He'd rather run down a wounded Impala over two full days than track an invisible enemy not of his own making. I know he'd rather walk away from this war in bare feet, drink water from the buried shells of ostrich eggs. His song is the song of a soul that longs for the earth as it was before it was cut up, fenced in and flogged from under his father's father's feet. The song stops. I look up from the fire. There is no sign of the moon anywhere. Just a cold sky covered in stars.
When I look back down, he too is gone.

•

Indaba, My Children: The bands had names - Khaki Monitor, Sons of Gaddafi Barmytzvah Band, Flaming Firestones, Corporal Punishment, Asylum Kids, Kalahari Surfers, Mapantsula.

Most of them played a club called Indaba Project in the heart of the city. It was one of a handful of places where whities and darkies danced together. Indaba had a roof garden with obstructed views of The Mountain on one side, the city and the smouldering Cape Flats on the other. Here people huddled under the stars with beers and joints and plotted the overthrow of the Regime.

(One night a tearful girl fantasized about obtaining a low-level job in the civil service: She would work hard until, after a few years and several promotions later, she would become the Groot Krokodil's‡ PA. Once there and near him day after day, she would poison him by spiking his morning coffee with tiny quantities of cyanide and watch as he slowly becomes more and more ill as the months drag by and finally die a painful death that would signal the beginning of the revolution...)

This was during another State of Emergency.
This was while army troops patrolled townships.
This was while there was only distrust between people.
This was while there were violent riots on many campuses.
This was while everybody whispered about the revolution that never seemed to come.
This was while people vanished off the streets, bundled into sleek cars with tinted windows.

...

Mad music droned in the club beneath our feet,
the city dozed and dreamed under an oblivious moon and
black mothers wept for their lost children inside dark shacks
and white mothers prayed in silence for the souls of their conscripted sons.

---

‡ *Groot Krokodil* – The Big Crocodile, nickname for P.W. Botha, 1916 – 2006. May he rot in hell.

Darth Vader, John the Baptist and a Dead Fish: I am the only punter in a Wimpy Bar. It is 1990. Late afternoon. Early spring. Not a breath of wind or a cloud in the sky. I stare out over an Atlantic at rest. Two cops enter, brush past and take the table directly behind me. Their presence makes me nervous. They smell like a State of Emergency. I wish they could go and sit somewhere else. Their uniforms are the blue-grey of interrogation rooms, boots like polished granite. Well-oiled 9mm pistols in holsters bulge on their hips. They order coffee. They smoke. They talk. I try not to listen. Their conversation drifts for a while, settles on, of all things under the sun, Darth Vader. Now I sit up, listen with intent. Darth Vader is their hero. Darth Vader is their station commander's nickname. Like Darth Vader, their station commander puts the fear of God into detainees and subordinates alike. They laugh at this. They laugh at how their commander can make a detainee piss himself by simply walking into the interrogation room. They laugh like school boys discussing a menacing headmaster. Then one of them notices a fish floundering in the shallows down on the beach. I look, spot the fish almost immediately. It flupps like a limp jewel. One of the policemen rushes outside, hits the beach at a dead run. Shells crush under his boots. The fish is trapped in the cusp between sand and water - gasping, gasping. Behind me the cop is cheering his colleague on. Down on the beach the hero stoops to scoop the fish up in his hand but pauses mid-action, straightens up again and looks up at his cheering friend, confused. The gasping fish at his feet is poisonous; it has spikes, not to be touched. He decides to attempt the rescue by nudging the fish into deeper water with the tip of his polished boot. The fish is slippery. It slides off his boot time and time again. Whenever he manages to nudge the fish back into the shallows the tide ejects it and the process starts all over again accompanied by cheering and goading from his buddy upstairs in the Wimpy. The rescue effort lasts maybe ten minutes with each attempt resulting in miserable failure. Eventually the rescuer throws in the towel, turns to his friend and shouts something about God's intentions or God's will. He returns to the table behind me, rejoins his laughing comrade, downs his cold coffee and lights an after-action-satisfaction cigarette. His boots have lost their sheen; they are wet and caked with sand and fish slime. Seconds later a *bergie*[§], profoundly drunk, ragged, staggers down the beach, locates the suffocating fish, scrapes it up with one hand and staggers back in the direction he came from. The fish fidgets a few more times in his grip and dies. Behind me the cops are silent. I smile to myself. The *bergie* appears inside the Wimpy Bar clutching the dead fish, heads for the grill section and tries to flog the fish to the duty cook, knocks over a display of condiments in the process of showing off his fresh catch. Bottles of secret sauce shatter. The cook laughs, calls over the manger. The manager is a big man with a small moustache and a Wimpy badge pinned to his white shirt. The badge proclaims: Hallo! I'm Anton. Have a Wimpy day! Anton grabs the *bergie* by his coat collar and marches him to the front door, shoves him out onto the promenade, back into the day. The *bergie* manages to stay on his feet through a combination of funky dance moves and the counterweight of the dead fish. *Let's Get Rocked* by Def Leppard kicks in over the PA. I watch the *bergie* meander down the beach. He plonks himself down in the sand and stays there staring at the fish and the ocean for a while. I watch as he struggles to his feet again, fish dangling limply from his fist. I keep watching as he heads straight for the water's edge and wades up to his waist into the freezing water. It looks as if he is whispering something to the fish. With a surprisingly smooth motion of the arm he lobs the dead fish into the air away from him. For a split second the fish is suspended against the sky. Then it turns on its own axis, completes its trajectory and hits the water tail first maybe five metres away from the soaked *bergie*. He remains motionless, eyes fixed to the spot where the fish splashed into the water hands clasped together below his chin. I think of John the Baptist. Then he turns around and wades towards the beach where he flops onto his back and just lays there drying in the sun. The policemen head for the door. At the door they greet Anton like an old friend, point towards the broken condiment bottles on the floor near the grill section in between hand shakes and back slaps. Anton shakes his head. The policemen leave. Anton doesn't charge them for the coffee. Back on the beach the *bergie* is sprawled on the sand like a holidaymaker. He is fast asleep. I try to spot the dead fish drifting in the glimmer. I cannot see it but I know it's there because seagulls are starting to hover over the spot where it hit the water.

I pay my bill and leave.

[§] Homeless person, male or female, (coloq.) Cape Town

Christel Re-entering Cape Town: He was taller than I imagined. • He looked fit and lean, holding Winnie's hand, waving at the crowd with the other. • New suit. Crisp shirt. Tie. • A hot day. • Sunday. Blistering. • A no-man's land wedged between past and future. • He looked like everybody's grandfather, didn't he? • We watched on TV as his motorcade snaked towards the city. • People lined the highway all the way from Paarl into town. • They cheered and laughed and waved as he passed. • During the afternoon, outside in the street, somebody shouted: *Christ is re-entering Cape Town!* • We walked down to the Grand Parade in front of City Hall to see/hear him for the first time in our lives. • Thousands sang freedom songs, pushed and shoved, sweated and cried. • Thick smell of cannabis, beer and flowers in the air. • Some people waved the crimsons of the SACP, everywhere the green, yellow, black of the ANC. • A boy danced with a wooden AK47. • I thought he dreamed of bullets, dreamed of bullets. • Clenched fists punched holes in the summer sky. • Cops from the Old Regime looked nervous and sweated, clung to their truncheons and thumbed their weapons. Their eyes darted in the darkness under their caps – eyes of animals cornered or criminals trapped. • Half the crowd chanted *AMANDLA!* And the other half replied *AWETHU!* • People scaled street lamps, swarmed a bronze of Jan Smuts like ants. • Some clawed their way into the date palms lining the square. • They chattered and fluttered like swallows. • A man with a Zionist Christian Church star on his lapel told me to *FUCK OFF* because *our time is come.* • I said *Ja, I know, I know...*and remained rooted to the spot.

Mandela held up his arms – a victorious boxer at the end of the 15th round. • A blessed silence settled over the square, the city, the sea, the world... • Then the voice, that voice none of us thought we'd ever hear. • And we thought it was over. • We thought we were saved.

Two Towns

1.

Saving You Time: A man in his thirties walks into the bar of the Swart Berg Hotel in Prins Albert and sits down next to me at the counter and orders a beer and a toasted cheese 'n' tomato sandwich. I can't remember what I was doing there or how I got there. He introduces himself. We start talking. He's the agent for Nashua Copier products for that entire region of the Karoo. He hands me a Parker ballpoint with *Nashua, saving you time, saving you money* printed down the side of it. Keep it, he says with a grin, I've got boxes full of 'em. I click the pen twice and pocket it. He says he's on the road a lot of the time and that he has to travel vast distances because the towns are so far apart. He loves driving. He loves his job. When I first started working the Karoo, I didn't have a company car, he says. I covered my turf in an old Kombi. The Kombi had a bed in the back and sometimes, on a deserted stretch, I would set the van up in the middle of the road, rest a brick on the accelerator, sit *lekker* on the bed in the back, and let the Kombi drive itself for a while. Later Nashua gave me a brand new Toyota Cressida with all the extras: aircon, automatic transmission, two-litre engine, automatic windows, cruise control, Pioneer radio/tape combo and a cup holder. That car made me love my job even more, he says. Like one afternoon, I was bombing down a laser straight road at about 140 k's, cruise control on, cig'ret going, Kenny Rogers Live full blast, both feet on the dash and I'm playing with the automatic windows. I was having the time of my life, hey. Suddenly I see a bend up ahead in the road. I panic. I try to flick the cig'ret in my left hand outa the window and in the rush get my fingers caught in it. This panics me so much I can't figure out which button lowers the *blerrie* window so I can free my hand to disengage the cruise control. The bend in the road is rushing towards me and my feet are still on the dash, hand caught in the window, and I swear to God, Kenny's crooning *The Gambler*. So, with my left hand stuck in the window, my feet on the dash, right hand on the wheel, Mr. Rogers and me take that bend at 140 on two wheels. I thought I wus gonna buy the entire fucking farm right there on that deserted road, I *tune* you, bra! After that I calmed down somewhat in my approach to self-entertainment out on those dull roads. These days, he says, I'd rather stop off for a cold beer and a toasted ham, cheese 'n tomato *sarmie* in the nearest town. Sometimes I'll pull off the road in the middle of nowhere and scour the veld for fish fossils or crystals for my daughter's collection. The Karoo used to be a ocean yonks ago, y'know. How freaky is that! Sometimes I'll climb the nearest *koppie* and strip off all my clothes and stretch out in the sun for an hour or two, make like I'm a lizard or a puff adder or a *dassie***. 'Point is I'm not so hell bent on anything anymore, y'know, getting from A to B and whatnot. What's the rush, hey? The Karoo is older than God. Our deadlines mean ab-so-lute-ly buggerall here. Time is meaningless here. Money too if you *skiem* about it. You might as well take your watch and chuck it out the window. Am I right or am I fuckin' right, china?

I wish I could recall his name.

** Cape Hyrax or rock rabbit

2.

White Man's Favours: Warrenton - another far-flung town. I strike up a conversation with the owner of the general store. He also owns the butcher shop down the road. His name is Barry. Barry is a bearded barrel of a man. Barry says he and his family are outcasts in Warrenton because of their *more relaxed racialistic views*. He invites me to his house for a *braai*[††] with his family later that night. I arrive. The house is big and squats on the edge of town. Beyond the house miles of flat space stretches as far as the eye can see. Bokkie greets me at the door. Bokkie is a one-eyed painter. He calls himself *Cyclops*, because *I can see and paint nothing but Truth*. His grin is a wall of yellow mealie kernels. I can't recall Barry's wife's name or the name of their pale young son. Bokkie hands me a cold Lion Lager, sits me down on a couch and screens his *art video*. His *art video* was created with a cheap video camera – a painfully slow panning shot and extreme close up of the surface of one of his abstract oils accompanied by a wild Frank Zappa number. I genuinely like the video. It is completely at odds with the landscape I can see through the open window directly to the left of the TV. The garish painting has no connection with the dehydrated landscape or the dusky horizon. Barry calls me outside. His son shows me the way. Nailed to a wall in a corridor near the back door I find a grouping of old framed portraits of bearded men and sullen women posing stiffly in their Sunday best. Among the portraits is a small photograph of a baby in a coffin. The baby is dressed in an ornate baptism dress. A date and a name scribbled in pencil in a corner of the photograph: Barend, 27 April 1918. *Who is this?* I ask the boy. *It is my dad's grandfather's brother. He died 3 months after his birth of the fever. It is the only photo of him we have*, he says and saunters towards the back door. Outside the fire is going. Barry pushes another Lion in my fist. Barry is turning huge steaks and sausage and fat hisses on hot coals like truck hydraulics. Later in the kitchen I am supporting my beery head in one hand, elbow on the counter. My fingers and lips are slick with animal fat. Bokkie is building a tower with the bones on his plate. His eye drifts like a juicy lychee in its socket. Barry is slurring his words. Foamy spittle shoots from his mouth as he speaks. He is going on about how *ungrateful* the *kaffirs* are, how they *simply do not appreciate what we've done for them when this entire dorp is so vrot*[‡‡] *with racialism*. Barry's wife tries to interrupt him with a *Ja but...*, but before she can utter anything coherent, Barry smashes his beer bottle on the floor behind him. Everybody around the counter freezes. Silence apart from the fizz of piss-warm beer on linoleum. The pale boy's eyes are big as ping-pong balls. Without even looking at his wife Barry says in a low voice: *Haven't we talked about this before? Hey? Do-not-fuckin'-interrupt-me-when-I-am-trying-to-tell-a-man-a-thing-for-fuckssakes*. Barry winks at me as if it is some kind of private joke I'm supposed to get. He asks if I want coffee. *Sure*, I say. Barry excuses himself, grabs his truck keys and says he'll fetch coffee from his store. Nobody says much while Barry's gone. I help clear the counter of plates and empty beer bottles. Barry's wife is on her knees picking up glass splinters and wiping beer from the floor and cupboard doors. Bokkie hasn't moved. He lifts a bone from the tower on his plate, sucks the marrow out of it and licks his fingers one by one. The pale boy is nowhere. Ten minutes later Barry is back with a small pack of Kloof Coffee. Kloof Coffee is cheap coffee. Chicory mostly. A poor man's brew. Barry holds up the small green pack like a trophy and says: *Ja, the white man's favours come in small packets, hey*. He laughs. Bokkie laughs. Barry's wife brews the coffee. I drink it black and bitter with a shot of Klipdrift brandy and leave before the mug is cold. Back in the motel room I lie on the bed in the dark and listen to the silence at the heart of the town. I think of the pale boy with the big eyes and Barry's silent wife. I think of smithereens of brown glass on a kitchen floor inside a house with a backyard as big as a country. I think of a one-eyed man who sees nothing. A baby in a coffin. The fever. The fever. I dream of hyenas ransacking dustbins in the deserted main drag of a war-torn town.

Their eyes glow yellow in the moonlight.

[††] barbeque
[‡‡] rotten, rancid

Itch: The car is about ten yards away, idling, lights switched off. I can just make out three people inside. I turn the corner and head for my house keeping an eye on the car. The guy in the passenger seat calls me over with a *Hey, whitie!* My first instinct is to keep walking but I'm too close to the car to pretend I did not hear him. I turn around and start walking towards the car. A wave of dread swells inside me. With every step I become more and more convinced the man in the passenger seat is going to blow my brains out as soon as I am close enough for him not to miss. Things like this happening all the time, every day. The papers are brimming with it. Bombs are going off all over the place: in student bars, in clubs. Even churches aren't safe. Nowhere is safe. No one is safe. Unrest everywhere. Old scores are being settled. History is coming home to roost. I keep walking. I know where the bullet is going to hit me. I can see how the man in the passenger seat slides a revolver from under his jacket. He points it at my chest, fires as the car pulls away. The bullet slams into my body and knocks me off my feet. I look down on my shuddering body sprawled on the cold tar, steam rising up from the blood pumping out of the bullet hole. When I finally reach the dark car I am numbed by fear. I can hardly stand. My mouth is dry. I steady myself with one arm on the car's roof, lean in towards the man in the passenger seat. He can't miss me now. Mirrored sunglasses cover most of his face and he is grinning up at me. He smells of beer. Perhaps it is the sour smell of my fear. His grin is wide. The Cheshire Cat. *Now*, I think, *this is It*. *Gizalight, my bra*, he says politely and produces a joint. I light it for him and they drive off. I stand with my lighter in my hand and watch the taillights vanish into the darkness down the far end of my street. I can't move. I can feel the ghost bullet itch inside my chest just below the heart - an itch I can't reach.

The Hissing Solace of Sprinklers: Eyes burn holes in my clothes the second I step

out of my car. People point at me and say things to their friends. They speak aloud because they know I can't understand them. I ask the nearest group where the *shebeen* is. They laugh like people who haven't heard a good joke in a while but point me down the street just the same. Dogs yowl and bark somewhere beyond makeshift shacks and breezeblock walls. The township smells of coal fires and wet dust. It is a foreign country. It is light years away from the soft suburbs with their jacaranda trees and clipped gardens and the hiss-hiss-hissing solace of sprinklers in the sultry afternoons. Women walk around with pails of water or large cardboard boxes filled with groceries balanced effortlessly on their heads. Wild gangs of barefoot boys swarm around me. They touch my clothes and sniff my skin. It is Lord of the Flies. There are bullet holes in the walls of a house, more in another. Dark alleys snake off in all directions. I might never find my way back home again. (A fantasy: a Xhosa family abducts me. I am their slave. After many years I manage to escape by which time I can't understand or speak Afrikaans or English any more – just like the white boy in a novel I read when I was a teenager – only, he was abducted by Zulus during the Great Trek. Back in my world, no one recognises or understands me when I try to tell my story...) The hubbub inside the *shebeen* subsides immediately as I walk in. It is a scene from a cowboy movie. The shebeen queen is gigantic. Her face shimmers like buffed ebony. I ask for Lion Lager. She points to a case of quarts and takes my money without saying a word. I don't hang around for my change. I can feel her eyes on my back as I turn to leave. Nobody else in the place even looks at me. I am a ghost, an untouchable, a curse. I make it back to my car with the crate of beer. I even make it back to the world I know.
A friend asks: So, how was it?
Cool, I say, cool.
I open a beer and watch a black gardener tilling red soil.
He sees me but pretends not to.
I offer him a beer.
He takes the beer. He smiles.
His smile is blinding.

Hiss-hiss-hiss-hiss-hiss...

Fuck You, Jake: It is a place where artists and yuppies and countless homeless men and women live cheek by jowl. It is the first night in the new house. I discover a man sleeping on the porch. I try to wake him up but he is too drunk to stir. He looks like a man made of mud and hair. He frightens my wife. Every morning he is gone. He returns late at night. Sometimes we can hear him drone a tune as he drifts off to sleep. We leave him alone. Over weeks his tattered belongings pile up in his corner of our porch. The pile reeks of shit and piss. It attracts flies. It attracts other vagrants. The stench invades our new house. I talk to him, reason, try to lay down rules. I learn his name is Jake. Jake is chaos on shaky legs. One night after a violent but bloodless brawl with one of his friends from the streets I tell him to leave. I watch as he slowly gathers his rank belongings and cross the street to set up house in a service alley. Jake's new address. Here Jake fucks and drinks, shits and snores and howls at the moon for the next few months. I have arguments with him. The neighbours have arguments with him. Jake stays put. One day Jake is gone. Over weeks his pile of stinking belongings vanish one object at a time until there is no sign he ever occupied the alley across the street. It is as if he never existed. I wonder what happened to him. I keep an eye out for him during my strolls through the neighbourhood. A season passes. Then another. I begin to forget Jake. We carry on with our lives. On a random autumn morning I step out of the house and see a dozen ragged people huddled together in Jake's alley. One of the women holds a plain cardboard cube with a lid. They are humming a hymn I do not recognise. The tune is cloaked in the clouds of vapour escaping from their mouths. I stand and watch. Hymn over, the woman with the cardboard cube lifts its lid and shouts: FUCK YOU JAKE, YOU CUNT, and chucks the chalky contents into the alley followed by the empty box. They pass a five-litre bottle of cheap white wine between them. They drain it and chuck the empty vessel into the alley where it shatters among Jake's chalky remains. They saunter off in the direction of the off sales leaving Jake to the wind.

Memory with Stop Signs

Wavering, pissed and hungry, he stands alone at
my door again.
I give him a sandwich, a blanket, coppers I find
in my pockets.
Without even trying to recall my name or a word for
thank you,
without a backward glance, he returns to the love
of no one.

How many times, I think later, listening to rain
on the roof,
has such a man, like any of us, taken a different path and found
only STOP signs?

Southern Discomfort

Fade in:

The shabby buildings look like they belong to some other city, not this one.

|Amsterdam maybe|

The wet streets shimmer with light.

|the streets in Taxi Driver|.|Maybe this is not real|

The liquor he ordered from the bar tender in the loud bar up the street
is now deep inside him, inside his brain cells,
bleeding through the walls of his veins into red flesh and
is dangerously close to oozing through tiny pores onto his skin.
It's a good feeling.

Light.

He's an essential part of the street like the cracks in the pavements,
the battered parking meters or the shrill party crowds he passes.
He catches the opal eyes of nymph-like girls wrapped in synthetic fabrics.
He can taste the tang of horny thoughts inside their heads,
smell fireflies in their eyes.
Faint whiff of designer cologne, designer drugs.

Most of the stores around here are junk stores
selling yesteryear to the here and now.

No bargains.

The past has become expensive.

A glowing window display:

Behind the window squats an ultramodern washing machine.
It looks out of place here in the old street.
White, ergonomic.
Bright and precise as a soap star's smirk.

He stares at it, at his reflection in the window superimposed over the machine.
The ultra-whiteness of the thing reminds him of the houses
high on the slopes of the flat mountain that looms over the city.
The houses are occupied by silky people, people who drive radiant 4x4's.

Their children are blonde and they seem to stay perfectly 11 forever.

His hair looks good.
Not too barbered, not too scruffy, incidental, casual like a lounge singer's from the 50's.
Sweat pearls just below the hairline on his forehead.
It's hot even for this time of the night, this time of the year.

He wonders if it is as cool and quiet on the inside of the white machine as it looks.
He wonders what it would be like to crawl inside the machine,
close the round door behind him,

shut the world out,
ride the spin cycle,
emerge clean.

He thinks of bourbon with lots of ice.

He strolls into a bar on the other side of the street.
It is crowded.
The air is moist with body heat and the dull drone of voices.
It smells of drunken laughter and crushed cigarettes and more being lit with Zippos.

|the open-and-shut click of a Zippo is a pistol being cocked|

The floor is sticky with countless spilled drinks.

He still feels good.
Alive.
As alive as he can possibly feel.

Awake.

-He imagines a hidden camera crew is filming him.-

He's the leading man in a movie.
As he snakes his way through the dense room everything becomes
slo-mo.
Only he knows he is being filmed.

He inhales the body heat of the *extras* around him.

The music is loud and cool like sweaty violence, seedy sex.
His clothes feel good on his damp skin:
Hawaiian shirt made of cheap tropical cloth that refuses to absorb sweat.

The dark pulse inside the music is a soft hand on his cock.

He reaches the bar and slams his hand down on its stained surface -
not so much for attracting the bar lady's attention
as for the pleasant burning sensation the action causes.
Behind the bar the light plays on the wall of bottles with their exotic labels.

He catches a glimpse of himself in the mirror behind the bottles.

|Nick Cage in Leaving Las Vegas|

The bar lady arrives.
She looks tired, harassed,
like this is only a temporary thing for her,
until something, someone better walks through the door,
something she can do while the sun shines, a knight on a white horse.

He orders Southern Comfort with lots of ice.
He watches her as she pours his drink.
Her body is on autopilot,
her mind is somewhere outside the room.

He imagines her sitting at the bar counter after all the punters had gone for the night,
marmalade light breaking in lines through the blinds in front of the windows facing the street.
She looks dazed, eyes fixed on a tiny score on the wooden floor between her feet ~

She deposits the drink in front of him with the passion of something
rolling off a production line or
a can dropping cold from a machine in an airport,
                                on a deserted station platform,
                                in a sterile hospital lobby.

|Obey Your Thirst!|

It is nothing more than the other end of a tired bargain:
this much money buys you that much booze.
It is clean, painless.
The ice comes free of charge.
So does the red napkin the drink rests on.

  ~This momentary lapse in the filming process is nearly enough to snap him out of it,
    but the fantasy is relentless, dogged ~

He pays for the drink, indicates for her to keep the change as she snaps up the brown note.
During all this she never looks him in the eye.

Not once.

He picks up his drink.
He likes the way the red napkin clings to the bottom of the glass.
He winks at himself in the mirror behind the bar then turns into the room,
leans back on the counter in a casual, filmic way.

He feels the light on the side of his face
and tries to imagine what it would look like
in close-up on a huge screen.

His back muscles are tight, tense.
His feet sweat inside his boots.
He feels dangerous, sexy,

        a time bomb.

Sweat snails down his spine, bleeds into his underwear.
His balls feel warm and moist.

He takes a deep swig of Southern Comfort,
rolls an ice cube around the inside of his mouth
before grinding it to water between his teeth.
The booze is sweet and comforting.

He slides the damp napkin from the bottom of his glass,
dabs the sweat off his face with it.
It changes colour, an even deeper red -
        fresh blood
or those drapes in whorehouses
in Sergio Leone movies.

He folds the napkin four times,
pinching the edges flat,
carefully, slowly.
He wants to know how to fold

origami monkeys,
        unicorns,
or   cranes.

|Edward James Olmos in Bladerunner|

He wants to be in Cuba or somewhere else far away from where he is.
      Anywhere.
He thinks of smoking a fat cigar,
white loafers on an old parquet floor,
an old car,
flashing neon above the door of a bar ~

Then he's back in the bar again.
Camera rolling.

He starts moving through the crowd.
The booze is a fist in the pit of his stomach.

The 90's sound track settles on the base of his skull like a cat.
He likes the feel of strange bodies brushing up against him.
He likes the feel of his shirt brushing over his damp skin,
chafing his nipples.

He stops in the centre of the room.
He lifts his face to the ceiling and closes his eyes.
It feels strange to be alive, to be here, now,
on the cusp of this Dark Continent.

He feels as modern as the music murmuring under the crackle of voices around him.
      ...Beats pierce his body like bullets...
The music is as new as the shiny white washing machine in the shop across the street.

He is millennial and tailor made for his time.

|Ralph Fiennes in Strange Days|

He wonders when he will get to see other places on the other side of the planet,
cities with streets older than the streets in this one.
He thinks of old bars with people speaking strange words
in strange tongues he wished he understood.

What about that guy in the TV ad who always looks
      so fucking smug and fulfilled
because of those Nikes he's wearing?

He thinks of the probabilities for- or against having a good life
and how he needs to sleep, sleep.
He thinks of the wet streets outside,
light melting red and amber and blue and green in them,
passenger jets slamming into the sides of gleaming skyscrapers on a flawless morning,
nuclear missiles exploding from secret silos hidden underneath waving wheat fields,
penetrating a woman from behind, back muscles rippling under her moist skin.
He thinks of the chaos inside the blood soaked morning papers,
the black turret of a nuclear sub ripping through ice,
four lines of shitty coke on a black toilet seat,
an eye being slit open with a straight razor,
bright flames spewing from dark oil wells,
the woman he once loved a long time ago,
a murdered friend's naked body next to a fucking motorway exit,
Porky Pig saying   *Th-th-th-that's all folks!*
a weeping woman holding a bleeding baby,
autumn leaves flaring on black branches,
a crocodile slithering into a murky river,
a bug-eyed boy holding a scuffed AK47,

his mother's soft hand on his cheek,
red dots on a green background,
dead children on Muslim streets,
a petrol bomb frozen in mid air,
birds floundering in an oil slick,
the Universal Pictures logo,
the Space Shuttle exploding,
the cancer in the seasons,
his dead dad's golf swing,
a beggar's open hand,
rows of riot police,
the cost of living,
a burning shack,
a fly on a turd,
cigarette,
blowjob,
AFRIKA!

Bright colours.

Darth Vader.

White noise.

Full moon.

Blizzard.

Hyena.

Heat.

ice.

!

BLACKOUT

Cape Town: A Place Abandoned

(After *Harlem: A Dream Deferred*, by Langston Hughes)

What happens to a place abandoned?

Does it crumble
like a structure swallowed by flood
or give in to war-
streets running red with blood?
Does it reek of neglect?
Or surrender to nature
like a dying insect?

Maybe it becomes bitter -
the mouth of a cheated lover.

Or does it recover?

Last Things

14th Avenue, Tshwane (née Pretoria?)

Time takes the heart of every thing. It has nothing to do
with you or the place. There is just the overness of it.
Every thing is still there. Yet nothing is left.

It is the same house in the same yard in the same street.
It is the same window. It is the same stream.
Yet the water in it is different water. That is all.

So, you saunter down the unsame street, past the changed stream,
towards the house where the overness of every thing sits and waits
in patient chairs, on restless beds, inside a cold kitchen

with cupboards vacant as caves and a saltshaker filled with nothing
but thirst. In every photo they still pose: Stiff-backed-bug-eyed,
cramped inside collars and bodices, confined

to frames: Men's men, ashy women, offspring in sailor suits.
No names. Your blood is their blood. Their marrow inside your bones.
Box-Brownie-stares seem to expect a real birdie to fly at them

in that blinding blaze between the whip of a shutter and the flutter
of eyelids. Beyond the window: the garden of good and milk, the land of evil
and honey where days still break as they always have: blood-orange red

behind bulky trees, black branches bending under wet weight
of unplucked fruits, rot slowly eating at the roots.
Yes, that unsame house under unchanged stars where

the sash window is the guillotine in your childhood dreams, where
numberless versions of you have stood in many shoe sizes, where
time broke in and took your heart and replaced it.

Preparation

Fling me once more into a blue sky and let me savour the momentary miracle
of wingless flight like a pint-sized Icarus with a bath towel cape
before you catch me in your arms

again. Explain to me once more the complex covenant between bees and flowers
and wipe the black stains of sun ripe mulberries
from my lips with your white

handkerchief. Show me once more that elusive turtle dove
in the looming cypress tree on the edge of the open plot
at the end of my boyhood

street. Buy me garish globes of cheap chewing gum from the rocket
outside the Greek corner shop with scrounged
copper coins from the folds of your jingling

pockets. Carve your face in the bark of my memory with your pocket knife
and carry me high on your shoulders
like you did when I was

five. Lob leisurely curve-balls at me just once more across a lawn dressed
in your shirtsleeves and loosened tie while we talk like men about our
clear-cut destinies and well laid

plans. Now, let me for once hold your hand and walk you for the last mile
or ten down this unbearable path before I let you slip
through the one-way doors of days.

Bunches of Bananas inside Boxing Gloves: He was never a tall man but he was solid as a Frigidaire. Strong hands, chunky fingers. Poor and rough, the youngest of fourteen, he used his hands to be heard. Twelve years old he beat the living shit out of an older boy - a snide remark about his shabby shoes. His pride broke the boy's nose and jaw, left him unconscious in the red dust. The attack was vicious, so bloody, gym-slipped girls screamed and fainted, crew cut boys went white and quiet and knew for the rest of their lives never to tease a poor boy about the holes in his soles. Shortly after this he took up boxing lessons at a youth club. Far more constructive, he said, than honing his swings and jabs like a hooligan on the streets. His thrift and thunder father grumbled about money and sin. His soon-to-be-dead-mother pinched pennies from the rainy day coffee tin for his boxing-lessons-on-the-sly. He smuggled his kit out of the house: vest and boxing shorts hidden under his regular shirt and trousers. Gloves, boots and bandages were stuffed inside a locker at the gym. He learned to skip rope for hours on end, days even given the chance. He gulped down stamina-enhancing breakfasts - raw eggs in glasses of milk before five-mile runs. After bouts he and his black and blue team mates walked down to the Hamburger Hut and placed their trophies on the counter for girls to admire. They celebrated their victories with cheese burgers and Cokes, conned wild American tunes from the Bel Ami with washers -

The Inkspots
Bill Hayley
The King
Little Richard
Louis Prima
The Cadets ...*And when I got to Lover's Lane I was almost*

   dead.
          But my soul was gone and here's what I said...

Back home he hid his trophies from his father under his bed.

A photograph of him circa 1952: Seventeen but somehow looking older. A clean-faced kid with jet-black hair Bryllcreemed flat against his head, green Everlast trunks shimmering like diesel in moonlight, soot black boots with laces white as crocodile teeth. Sunburnt legs strong as bridge supports, the body barrel hard, compact, teen-toned. He wears the white vest of an amateur, his bunches of bananas hidden inside boxing gloves. The eyes are roofed by a unibrow. They blaze with the vim and vigour of pugilists past –

Fullmer
Graziano
Turpin
Louis
LaMotta
Sugar-Ray

His gaze punches through the glass and the frame and seems to reach beyond the curve of his future. In that photograph my father-before-he-was-my-father is every man at the start of his life, ready to take on, beat to a pulp, and break the jaw of anything that might get in his way. But in the final round, like all of us, he took swings at shadows, lost on points.

Stones

"It does no good to wave my arms."
                    -Sam Shepard, Cruising Paradise-

On the last day of the year, while I hacked the head off a dying pigeon
in the garden, you were wrapped inside a warm blanket on the couch,
quivering, a stranger shrunk to the size of a boy.

The next day you were up, miraculously man size again, sitting behind
your desk in your cluttered study - mom always moans about the chaos -
reinventing your life story from your maimed memory.

You found it easier to write about yourself than to talk about us.

Why was there a bloodless silence between us? (*A silence between men
is a silence between stones.*) Was it because you always preferred
chit-chat, talk about the mundane, the practical, the skin-deep:

Politics, the economy, the price of petrol, Rugby scores, my day so far?
Or was it because I always refused to talk for the sake of talk,
unless it was about the marrow of a thing?

Blood will run where words don't flow.

Over the weeks I sat - always in bloody silence - and watched you page
and page through two broad sheets a day, reading nothing,
taking nothing in, just the habit of handling a paper.

Or I watched as you turned the same paper over
and then over again - a lost man trying in vain
to locate himself among the contours on a map:

Front page, sports page, front page, sports...

When you finally spoke, you spoke to nobody in particular,
mumbled something about blood and imminent disaster, violence,
lack of clear communication and how the story never seems to change.

I opened my mouth to agree, disagree, offer you coffee, something,
anything, but no words would form. Later, over a glass of wine, I pointed
at the spot in the garden where I'd buried the pigeon and you nodded and said:

Where a bird dies there is always feathers.

The next day two more newspapers arrived.

Last Days of the Comeback Kid

During the last months, they said
the Comeback Kid stopped reading newspapers,
left them untouched and neatly folded
next to his easy chair like a pile of fresh table cloths.
They said, during the last weeks,
the Comeback Kid lost all interest in hunger and thirst,
ignored sustenance as if he was a holy man fasting for insight.
They said he lost all sense of place, time, space,
that he became a drifter, a man adrift, flotsam.
During the last days, they said,
the Comeback Kid slept almost nothing, emerged at noon,
a retired boxer who'd had his fill of fights.
They said the Comeback Kid became a man of halves:
half asleep, half awake, half sad,
half interested, half there, half not.
By the last day, they said,
the Comeback Kid was made of wispy things:
skin rice-paper-thin, hair of cobwebs,
limbs brittle as drift wood, leaf-flat body, reed-thin voice.
Then, in his final hour, there were the last quivers,
breath the sound of a canned blizzard.

And during the last minutes, I imagine,
the Comeback Kid became his own shadow,
blue eyes black as squid's ink,
arms flung open like a skydiver frozen in free-fall,
a landscape gathering darkness at the end of a day.

Departure – Fourteen Variations

14
it did not come without warning
      merely a long delayed train arriving late
or
sooner than expected

13
     last things
unsaid words piled high
      bags of undelivered mail on a platform
gestures intended but never executed
     all meaning lost
&
the technology of longevity
     machines designed to prolong hope beyond hope

12
something bleeps & breathes
        with unnatural regularity
no human is capable of

11
what it comes down to is this
        this is the end of the line

10
hand twitches
tiny muscle in an eyelid
     eye behind it moves
        a mouse in a bag
searches out a pinpoint of light

                          a way out

9
lips slightly apart
breath escapes
     a faulty seal
     soothing as a gas leak

8
lines on the face

                         old roads

no signposts or mile markers

                         i get lost

bedside lamp is the only star in the sky

                         where to?

7
impressions of his feet still in the carpet
      fossilised footprints
where he always stood staring down days
      birds cracking seeds
the garden he wrestled from scorpions & snakes
      pulling at grubs

6
walk miles in the room
level walls looking for a straight _____line
that can lead me

                                        away from here

5
count floor tiles again   again
        forget the number
          odds or evens
          sixes or sevens
as soon as i am done counting

4
track the second hand on his discarded watch
on its jerky journey around the black face
next to it a glass of water
                    short straw

3
think
odd how time & water mean so little
here
now
in this room

think
how little symmetry
distance   between   walls
dimensions of rooms
colour of sheets
names of days
lengths of months
sports scores
tv schedules

timetables

life death
my age his
mean in the face of this

                        thing

2
here all text is robbed of subtext
time of length
eyes of sight
minds of thought
conversations of words

1
him & i
        father & son

                now & now

0

Brando...Fat and Dead

It's almost time.
/
What's to say at a moment like this? It was good to have you here? Don't be a stranger? See you soon? Thanks for everything? Bon voyage? Godspeed?

Christ. Time. It's seldom long or short enough.

It's just...I don't know...we talked and talked...and nothing seems...maybe too much water under the bridge...too much time. Too many clichés. You and I. / We should've done this sooner, talked, years ago. Then again, there is always one more thing to say, so...
///
Time// It bends the mind. Things become...skewed over time. Things crack open. Shatter. Smithereens. There are things... just...splinters of things inside my head. Things I wanted to tell you, things I remember. Things I think I need to remember. But it's also *how*...I seem to remember things, how we all remember things, I guess. Maybe it's the same for everyone. I don't know how it's supposed to work though, the act of recall, how we're supposed to know if something, an incident, is remembered correctly, recalled accurately as it were, you know, if it's really true, what you remember, if it is really your own memory. Real. I mean; is it a story somebody told me of something *they* remembered? Did I see it in some movie long ago and it somehow ended up slowly bleeding into my real memories up to the point where I think it is something that actually, definitely happened to me? But then you find some thing just won't fit. Some little detail, a chink in the surface. You obsess for days on end, checking the details, trying to separate fact from fiction, doing your best to glue it all together, picking it apart again like a knot, running and rerunning it in your head like an old home movie, a slide show of some kind. You start putting names to faces, pick a day of the week, a season to hang it all on. You write the dialogue, who said what. Intonations. Hesitations. Maybe a fleeting look in the eyes, a tiny gesture. A location: Did it take place in a room, a park, inside a car next to the ocean, at a station, an airport parking lot, a motel lounge, the schoolyard, inside a lift between floors, at a police station? You know, things like that. How old were you? Was it night or day, morning, afternoon, raining, hot? What songs were cool at the time? TV shows. And then one day, out of the blue, you run into the lead character in this memory of yours. You're leaving someplace and this person is just arriving or something. You haven't seen each other in fucking ages. You sit down somewhere. You're talking and catching up and then you say: "Listen, before you go..." And you describe this jumbled memory to this person and it turns out he or she can't remember this vitally important moment in your life at all. Or they weren't even there. Jesus! That really fucks with your day, don't you think? / Sorry. I didn't mean to...

Now, this is funny. I just remembered this. When I was much younger, a boy, I was convinced that long ago, long before I was even born, maybe even before you were born, you know, the world used to be black and white like in old photographs. I believed the world looked like those pictures of granddad when he was a young man or the ones of you and mom when you were just married, walking on a promenade somewhere eating ice cream. / Or like the old movies we watched on TV every Friday night, us kids sprawled on the carpet under a blanket...or was it Wednesday nights? Anyway, it doesn't really matter. It was a million years ago. The point is I was convinced, completely, utterly convinced of this. I even believed there was a time when every person on earth, every creature moved really fast like Chaplin and I couldn't work out why nobody else noticed it, mentioned it in history books, or when things started mellowing out a little, became, well, 33rpm instead of 78. // Look, I know it makes no sense at all. It's just one of those weird things kids work out for themselves while they're fighting off sleep, listening to the strange adult noises in the house or trying to ignore the howl of the wind through a tree outside. Then you grow up and you realise the absurdity of these notions that seemed so clear, so fucking, sorry, so convincing to you back then. But our minds somehow never really give up on those theories. We're never willing to let go of them, not completely, sell them out to cold reality, to the adults we're supposed to have become. Maybe this is because they were too hard won. They are much more interesting than the truth anyway...reality. // I don't know. ///

A friend of mine once told me how, as a little girl, she was so impressed with herself to have a boy called Paul as her best friend. Why? Because she was convinced there was a special Christmas carol just for him, as in: *"Silent night. Holy night. PAUL is white, PAUL is bright..."* A guy I know believed for the longest time God's name was Harold, you know, *"Our father which art in heaven, HAROLD be thy name..."* And both these people say they still believe those things; that Paul has his own Christmas carol or that God's name is Harold even though it makes no sense. You see? Sense doesn't stop us from wanting to check under our beds or inside our closets from time to time for demons or monsters before we switch the lights off, does it? Sure, not many of us actually check our rooms and the dark corners in the house before we go to bed, but it's there nonetheless, that impulse, that tiny voice whispering in our ears.
// Bizarre. / Don't you think?
...

So, in the same way I still believe this thing about a long-lost black and white world when men looked like men and cities were new and streets were clean and when everybody scuttled around like rats on acid. // I envy you for having had the opportunity, the good fortune for having known such a time, for having experienced a world like that, a monochrome world, a world with a little mystery left in it even though I know full well you never lived in a world like that. Not for real anyway. The world was never black and white. It was never as cut and dried as I always needed it to be. /

Liz Taylor looked so much better in black and white, don't you think? Now she's so...I don't know...she's...and Brando...fat and dead. // I've never been any good at coping with colour at all. Hurts the eyes. Does that make any sense to you? /// Probably not. /

You've always been so level headed, pragmatic. Is that even the right word? Prag-ma-tic? Practical? Sober? Thing is, you tried your best to keep things real for me and I never woke up, not completely. I just kept on dreaming and now I'm here...with you...talking ...waiting. //

Sometimes, on days like today, I catch myself wondering when exactly the big switch to colour happened. I mean, was it slow like wine bleeding into a tablecloth? You see, in my mind it happened extremely slowly over many, many years, decades and nobody really noticed, in the same way nobody notices a creeper covering a wall or how monkeys turned into humans. I don't think everybody simply woke up one morning back in the fifties or sixties or forties or whenever it happened and, BAM, the world was not black and white anymore. The shock would've done people's heads in. / Ridiculous. //

I guess my point is...all I really want to say is...shit...I don't know now.

....

I constantly feel like I'm in a Buster Keaton movie and I'm the only one standing still...and...yet... /

Look, I know we don't have long, but let me just say this one last thing: I think all we are, all we have, are moments. Moments that burn themselves into the neurons deep inside the brain, vanish into the hippocampus. A moment. This moment. This, here. Everything. That is it. Don't you see? This is all we have. This is all you and I will ever share, all we ever had. Everything, our whole world, our entire lives can change in a single moment. Perhaps even in this very moment we are in, or the next. A moment can change everything. / Just like that. One warped memory, one wrong move, a word out of place. Nothing left. Things change. Always. It's never-ending and it seldom makes any sense at all. I think *you* told me that. But I can't be sure. Sometimes things change slowly, sometimes too fuc..., too bloody fast, in a blur, between blinks. So there is no truth. Not really. There can't be. The mind bends things. We bend things. Time bends things. It bends us, runs out on all of us. Every time. All these moments, gone. Our lives. So all there is is you and I, here, now. There can be nothing else. //

Hey, in time, who knows, neither of us might remember any of this, right? It will be as if none of it, here, now, this conversation, today, ever happened. Or worse: Only one of us will think he remembers this moment and the other one won't have a clue what he's on about. So, I guess my point is I don't have a point. I needed to see you one more time before you have to leave and...

This is it then. // Take care, OK? / Thanks... for everything. For listening. Always listening. For being there, here, for me.

I won't forget it. / I won't forget you. / Ever. / I promise. //
Come / give us a hug.

Dictum

You leave the room,
set off down the street,
burning history as you go.

      The room becomes meaningless.

We all have to get used to meaningless rooms:
gleaming wooden floors creak with old age,
the day's fragrant warmth loiters in the desolation.

      Desolation can be so peaceful.

I look out through a window:
leaves forming, trees more lush, more moist,
flaming with compassion and feminine abundance.

      Abundance does not spread, famine does.

One day I'll trip on the windowsill,
fall into the street, spread-eagled in the dust,
one day, when I'm bored with god's blue sky.

Rain Mask

Remember the first time I laid eyes on you?

      Was it a hot afternoon?

Did you appear at the top of the stairs in that house on the slope of the mountain,

      the house you shared with your boyfriend?

Was there an African mask on the wall behind you as you stuck out your hand

      to greet me?

Were my first words to you "I love your mask"?

Did you reply "Yes, it is extraordinary. It is from the Ivory Coast. I collect masks.

That one is for making rain. We sure need rain. You can have it if you like."?

      Did I fall in love with you there and then?

      Did I take the mask when I left that afternoon?

If I did I must have lost it or left it hanging on a wall in a room

inside a house I abandoned some time ago.

I am sorry.

I should have made rain for us.

Rake This

I wrote:
Happy 1st birthday to the kid!
Love,
G.

It took you five days to reply:

Happy day! One year in the world!
Climbs the stairs. Walks like a drunk.
Terrorises the cats. Speaks fluent Mandarin.
Love,
C.

Mandarin?

I play with the word: Man-da-rin,
Roll it around like a marble in my palm,
Put it in my mouth; let it loiter on my tongue.

I return to your reply to look for clues between the lines:
Three simple lines like a neatly raked tomato patch.
Not a single stone for turning or a leaf for pruning.

Six days later I reply:

C,
Rake this patch:
She stands in a small grove behind a double storey house,
Speaking the complex language of oranges to two terrified cats.

G.

Last Reel (American Ending)

And night did a slow cross-fade into day as we hit the road, headed for the river.
You picked Nick Cave and the Bad Seeds as the music for the opening sequence.
Music for reprobates and clueless saints, you said, squeezed my leg, winked and grinned.
So, halfway there we stopped off at the Shell Ultra City *(Hell Ultra Shitty)* for breakfast:
double cheese 'n' bacon burger, chips and awful coffee for me,
for you sensible over-easy-eggs on whole wheat toast, tea.
Then more coffee to go-go and three carrier bags of munchies, cartons of Camel Plains.
You bought Nu Car Smell, a Wigglin' Elvis for the dash just for the hell of it
and because you knew he'd make me laugh every time we hit a bump in the road.
Then you, me and The King rock 'n' rolled out of there with a fresh tank of gas,
aimed north for the mountains, the river and out ran the old year in the rear-view mirror.
Like Sheen and Spacek in Badlands we were already far off the map.

(Fade to black)

And I swear you set that entire river ablaze all the way down to the Atlantic
every time you dipped your crimson Cutexed toes in the water,
making schools of baby salmon scatter like freaked children.
One afternoon we dropped acid and you rolled King Size Rizla joints,
just like that ex boyfriend taught you during your "extended stay" in Amsterdam.
And I thought I'd lost my mind tuning in to the psycho-thoughts inside the heads
of a troop of baboons casing us with red eyes from a nearby outcrop.
But you cradled me in the water like I was a sinner, the river a Holiday Inn swimming pool,
and you calmly reassured me with a *shhh* that all's well, that none of it was real
apart from the arc of the sun, the curve of sky, the burning river and us.
But in my head we'd become Matt Dillon and Kelly Lynch in Drugstore Cowboy.

(Fade to black)

And at the end of that summer we headed back to the city in silence.
Through the bug-splattered windscreen the New Year stretched ahead of us,
an endless black prairie we somehow knew we'd never cross.
So we drove bullet straight into a back-lot sunset as the final credits rolled:
Anti-heroes at the end of a B-movie with nothing left to say for the rest of their lives.

(Fade to black)

Orphaned Latitudes

Leave your land and you leave yourself.

Unknown

Third Dispatch

Date: Fri, 11 Aug 2006 00:59:21 +0000 (GMT)
From: "Gerard Rudolf" <gerardrudolf@yahoo.co.uk>
Subject: A Dog Life Anyway
To: "FE" ********@yahoo.com

F,

What is Joburg like? It's vibrant and aggressive. It is unflinchingly African and brutally beautiful. Since 1994 the city has become a crazy melting pot, a Babel of all Africa's languages and cultures. Congolese men with sharp haircuts and insanely beautiful traditional shirts hang out on street corners. Sharp featured Ethiopians sell their silver jewellery from sidewalk stalls. Zulu women in bright dresses and complex headgear walk around in small groups with babies tied to their backs or sit straight legged under acacia trees chattering like birds. Nigerians leer at you with simmering violence from flashy cars bought with drug money. They swear at each other in fast Yoruba, dress like American rappers - all Nike and bling. Everywhere one can pick out the ragged Zimbabweans with the hardship of illegal border crossings and fear of deportation behind their tired eyes. There are the smoothies from the Ivory Coast, grinning Kenyans as black as coffee, their teeth Colgate white in the sun. They are all in Joburg. Outside the city's trendy hotspots expensive cars throb with the sex soaked beats of Kwaito music. Inside the post-modern shopping malls of Rosebank and Sandton City the new African middleclass shop Prada, Diesel, Rolex, Gucci, Hugo Boss. They drive BMW, Porsche, Mercedes and spotless 4x4's. They lounge in sidewalk cafés sipping espresso, cappuccino and fruit juice under a summer sky stacked high with clouds. They pick at International Cuisine and sushi while they calmly watch the world blur by from behind dark Raybans. They smell of Chanel No.7 and CK1. They talk politics and business. Crime is discussed like it's the weather. They rub shoulders with nervous milky Scandinavian, German, Japanese, American and British tourists; watch them spend their £'s and €'s and ¥'s and $'s with sly smiles. Just a few feet away their illegal refugee brothers and sisters hawk sidewalk art, bright beads, traditional cloths, bin liners, cheap Chinese toys, pirate DVD's, coat hangers and cell phone peripherals at traffic intersections where frightened white people try hard to ignore their relentless sales pitches behind firmly locked car doors. In Joburg carjacking is the national sport, smash-and-grab the latest craze. Rich, poor, homeless, jobless, haves and have-nots mix uneasily in the sultry summer heat because they have no alternative other than simply to get on with the New South Africa – no matter what Mbeki said about the so-called "African Renaissance" or AIDS. Centuries of distrust between black and white still run under the pavements like dark streams. The streets hustle and bustle while new buildings shoot up all over the place right next to inner city ghettos where even the cops don't dare enter. Pockets of grinding industry are separated by large no-go zones. Scarcely a decade ago the old Joburg city centre was still a place of gleaming skyscrapers, banks, mining companies, Art Deco apartments, the stock exchange, shops, parks and 5 star hotels like the Carlton. Now the skyscrapers and hotels and shops and apartments are for the most part abandoned or taken over by slum lords who rent space without water or electricity to the poorest of the poor – sometimes fifteen souls to a room. (I heard a beggar say: "It's a dog life anyway...") Where family businesses once thrived there are now cheap clothing stores and African muti shops with wild herbs, animal body parts hanging from the ceiling and strange ointments in old jam jars. The government is constantly talking of "regenerating the city centre" but nothing seems to happen. Meanwhile in the city's leafy suburbs the kitsch mansions of the new rich cower behind high walls and automatic gates and armed response teams in American style uniforms patrol the jacaranda-lined avenues day and night. The sound of house and car alarms and barking guard dogs has become the second national anthem after Nkosi Sikelel' iAfrika. Overloaded minibus taxis race each other on Joburg's concrete highways ferrying workers into the city from dusty townships like Soweto, Alexadria, Thembisa. They have to be fast because time is money and life is cheap. They call the taxis "Zola Budds" after a famous South

African long distance runner who ran with bare feet, who accidentally tripped an American athlete during some race at the LA Olympics back in the 80's. In Joburg Africa meets World head-on while America builds its walls and Europe crouches in its own moral shit. Joburg has her arms and legs wide open as Baghdad burns and China flexes her muscles. Joburg is a frontier town without a sheriff. Joburg is a future-shock-vision of the world. She shouts at you in police sirens, gunshots, paranoia and traffic jams. Oversized billboards advertise Microsoft, Impala Maze Meal, Nokia, Sony, Nissan, Five Roses Tea, Riccoffee, Castle Lager and Surf washing powder (here an image of a smiling young black house wife holding up a clean sheet with the legend "MAKES YOUR WHITES EVEN WHITER!" Nobody seems to notice the irony). The billboards blare their middle class aspirations at everyone from the slopes of mountain-sized mine dumps dotted all over the landscape. Joburg stinks of old history, new money, past glory, New Freedom, creativity and real Human Issues like AIDS, housing, poverty, corruption, survival, murder, mayhem, culture clash, violent crime, affirmative action, easy money, hunger and baby democracy. In Joburg a loaf of bread is political. Who cares if the trains never run on time? Who cares about the alarming murder rate or if houses are burgled and cars are 'jacked? Joburgers are a tough breed. Joburg, Josie, Igoli, Gauteng, J'town is a toddler with a loaded gun doing pirouettes on the edge of chaos. It is a fucked up, wounded place, beaten black and blue by history.

Some say Joburg is a suburb of hell.

I don't know.

You should go and see.

You'll hate it then, perhaps, love it.

From the Mouths of My Mother's Sheepskin Slippers

Now the African winter is spent like a salary,
sounds will swell like a new tide.
Nomadic birds will return breathless to roost,
and colours will find their destined objects.

                            I could sit like this forever,
here in my dead father's weather-beaten wicker chair,
listen to this small garden skelter
with new, invisible life: all around me leaves
sprout, things move, crunch, drip, mutate.

On the inside too something begins to stir
and split open like a new-ploughed field.
It murmurs and pulses in the cerebral cortex -
a bee droning deep inside a humid hive.

Then the notion rears its head, a snake in the grass -
briefly: the last to go with my final breath
could be a word, but now I fear silence
might throttle me and leave me grasping at voids.

                         But your sheepskin slippers yawn
at me from their perch in the sun. Their Black Mouths
tell me my body's always where my mind is not,
to live my life with my mouth firmly shut,
and my eyes, my eyes, my eyes agog.

Dig for New Shoes

"Doth the moon care for the barking of a dog?"
        - Robert Burton, Anatomy of Melancholy (1621), pt.II, sec.III, mem.7.

On the Day of Departure

    I bury my old shoes in the dust of my fatherland.
    I lick the soil and inhale the grumbling thunder clouds;
    They loom heavy over the veld like omens bad or good.

    On the last night I hear the yowl of dogs over drowsy suburbs.
    Near the airport I spit at the monuments of times 'great' and 'fair'.
    I trawl the departure hall for duty free reasons to stay.

During the Flight

    I dream I shuffle my bare feet to the beat of township jive.
    I taste blood at the root of history, spew flames from dark veins.
    Spit-polished saxophones wail like trancing sangomas[§§].

    I dream I plunge my face into the icy ocean of my motherland.
    I drink her stingy rain and curse her oblivious moon:
    It swells ripe behind a flat mountain, solid as insomnia.

Upon Arrival

    I declare the itch of memory and bewilderment.
    I produce the bitter dog that devours its owner.
    Dig for new shoes in the mud of a strange land.

[§§] sangoma(s) - traditional healers, soothsayers, holy men/women, South Africa.

Overnight Commercial Flight

At 34 000 feet I dream with eyes wide open:
An air disaster – human limbs and unclaimable
luggage hang from the jungle canopy like ripped laundry.
Securely strapped to my seat (21D) and in the impact position,
the smell of aviation fuel, blood and crushed cherimoya trees
lull me to sleep among the chaos and shrapnel
of 20th century engineering, haemorrhaged wiring,
tourist trinkets, complimentary peanuts and fucking ready meals.

Africa is restless, restless at night.

At 3:45 a.m. I am still awake with eyes firmly shut.
Inside my head I water old thorns for the sake of flowers,
and hold my breath as we cross the equator
from South to North – an old spice carrying clipper
on return from the Old New World to the New Old World.
But sudden turbulence jerks me back to the 21st century,
forces recycled air from my nicotine-starved lungs
and I think of the small black box that won't record
my exquisite modern annihilation after all.

Africa seems endless, endless at night.

43 Objects Confiscated From Me by HM Customs at Heathrow at 6am on a Sunday Morning

1. I hate you more than a fleeing man hates his passport checked.
2. I am as small as all small things when you look me in the eye like that.
3. Being in a hurry won't prevent us from dying – neither does going slow prevent us from living.
4. I love this hour of wind and light.
5. The heart is cast of human cares and joys.
6. Candles toppled sideways inside old tomato cans.
7. Sleepless on the night flight. Through the porthole, shuddering stars. *The universe is nervous*, was all I could write.
8. She will know of a cheap release.
9. If you give me hunger, what then do I owe you?
10. We spent a baker's dozen years joined at the hip. Now I don't even know where you live.
11. My mother said I came out of the blue, a guest arriving long after they'd stopped expecting me.
12. Another person's heart is a wilderness.
13. She came running to him around noon:
Daddy! I want to drink the rain and eat the moon!
14. Now there are strangers on our lips.
15. For what is hot, the spoon,
For what is cold, the hand.
For who is lost, the moon.
16. Early to rise, early to bed, nothing left to say, adventure is dead.
17. If May could talk, it would brag it invented romance. South of the equator October could say the same thing.
18. Try and explain this to a British cop: White African of Dutch, French, German stock,
When all he wants is to tick a little box.
19. You can't take the day with you.
20. The mind can only stand what the arse can endure.
21. I'll sift through the detritus of travel, and end up throw nothing away.
22. Black scrawl on a toilet wall: *Bono, I want to see the world through your eyes!*
23. Our capacity for experience is far greater than our capacity to understand. We blithely survive on paradoxes.
24. I wish I could recall who said: night is a shoal of black fish sprinkled with sea salt.
25. Your body was a faraway nation. Now I have the stamps in my passport.
26. Pride only goes as far as you can spit.
27. I keep blowing the flute on the wide side.
28. If you don't believe in signs you can't live in this world.
29. I want to draw a map of what is effortless.
30. God provides abundant nuts for the toothless.
31. An Asian boy with a Buddha face wearing a t shirt with the legend: Martial Artist.
32. Almost is not eaten.
33. The underdog is always full of dreams.
34. When there is nothing left to burn you have to set fire to yourself.
35. I am a man of North and South / One foot in Europe / the other lodged in Africa / My balls dangle in the cold Atlantic / The African sun shines out of my arse / I'm easily the tallest fucker in any room /almost every time.
36. My grandfather stands in a wheat field up to his belt, hat half-cocked, slightly turned up nose - a scarecrow powerless against crows - Just a man standing, a man contemplating the miracle of bread in a country where a loaf is as political as Apartheid's dead.
37. The man over there, sitting on his suitcase, is a haiku to departure or a novel about arrival.
38. Understand the start and the end won't surprise you.
39. I catch myself saying things like 'mate' instead of 'bru', 'lovely' instead of 'lekker', follow statements with 'to be honest', greet people with 'alright?' instead of 'howzit?'
40. Alone is only good for going to the toilet.
41. See the beauty and you won't notice the difference.
42. The day you told me my eyes are cowards.
43. It's a bad decade for love.

Memory/Atom

The trees on the other side of the road somehow shed their leaves over
the past few days. Their branches stand out against the monochrome
sky like medical charts mapping veins
entering lungs -

their elephant skins are blackened by soaking rain sifting down
on them for the past two days. There is a nip inside the wind,
a chill infused with the ice of the North Pole,
I think -

its frigidity makes my African bones rattle and shudder,
activates weird enzymes deep inside my solar plexus.
They carry messages of warning to
my brain -

pedantic memoranda to remind me that I am not from here,
that my ancestors have been away from these latitudes
for far, far longer than any atom in my body
can recall.

Two Hands: On the first day of a three-day hike, in the early afternoon, I pick up a perfect specimen of rose quartz the size and shape of a pigeon egg. I roll it in my hand as I walk. The hiking party is heading west along the river. To the north of the river, beyond the steep canyon wall is Namibia and thousands of miles of ever-increasing waterlessness. To the south lies the semi-desert-flatness of the Northern Cape. The river is deep and wide. It forms a perfect barrier between two countries. There are stories of wild men crossing this river on horseback long ago and were never seen or heard from again. I have read accounts of killer gangs who roamed these parts during the 19th century preying on trekkers fleeing the liberal laws of the British colony at the Cape, killing the men, raping the women and making off with their children and threadbare belongings. This place has never been tamed. The river is the colour of desert sand. It compliments all the hues of the landscape around it – brown, muted green, black, grey, ochre. Above it all, a cloudless sky. Unlike us in our synthetic fabrics, heads lodged solidly inside cities and the acoustics of flux, the river belongs here. The river follows its own course. We have to follow the river. The river is quiet. Only boulders cutting through her murky surface like half submerged heads break her silence momentarily. The going is tough. Nobody talks. I keep thinking about the age of the river. I am never at ease. I heard troops of baboons patrol parts of the river canyon. A male baboon can rip a man's arms off if it feels cornered. Baboons are psychopaths and this is their realm. I walk on. Thoughts eventually fall away. All that remains are my burning muscles, the sweat bleeding into my hatband and the grind of my boots on rough river gravel. Dusk. We build a fire. Tinned food is cooked, coffee. Night falls, muted conversation. Later, only stars and the restless rustle of bodies cocooned inside sleeping bags. I can't sleep. I suspect nobody sleeps. I listen to the river, the hiss and crack of the fading fire. I track shooting stars across the sky with my index finger. I warm the rose quartz egg in my hand. Dawn and we follow the river again, let her flow drag us along. We scuttle through thorny thickets, wade waist deep through water where the trail vanishes against insurmountable obstacles; toppled boulders the colour of elephants, ripraps of twisted stumps and branches. We drink ice-cold water straight from the river. In the afternoon I hear baboons barking somewhere in the canyon up ahead. I am too tired to care. Communication is down to single syllables during rest stops. Dusk again. Fire. Food. Night. No sleep. Cold. Red dawn burns the river. Walk. Follow the river. We have no idea where we are, how far we are from the pickup point. Our maps are useless. We stop and haggle over landmarks but nothing is where it should be. Every peak, every outcrop, every bend in the river looks the same. We push on. We have no choice. I pull away from the group. Midmorning: I almost bump into a man and a woman walking in the opposite direction. The man wears a threadbare suit the colour of the landscape. He is barefoot. His hat is held together with sweat, dust and a snakeskin band. The woman is in a bright summer dress with a grimy lace collar. She is also shoeless. The three of us simply stare at each other. They both carry the raisin features of the Khoi San. They are tiny, maybe 5 feet tall from crown to toe but perfectly proportioned. They belong with the river. They belong to the land. They are the landscape. They are her children and the river is their sister. I can sense this. Their ancestors left their riddles and signs on overhangs and inside the shallow caves of this place more than thirty thousand years ago. Where were our ancestors then? The man smiles at me and I smile back. I ask him in Afrikaans how far it is to the pump station, our pickup point. He removes his hat and stares directly into the sun. His eyes narrow. It looks as if he is divining an answer from the sun, listening to a voice from beyond the blue of the sky. His eyes are slits in raw hide. With his eyes fixed to the sky he answers my question:

Miskien minne as 'n oggend as djy vinnag loep. Ma' dalk oek'ie heelmirrag as djy sloer.
(Maybe less than a morning if you walk fast, maybe a whole afternoon if you walk slow.)
Yes, but how many miles?
Twie'hanne of soe. (Maybe two hands or so.)
Ten?
Ja, assit minner is as 'n dag. Nie verrie. Nie naby'rie. Seintoe. Af merrie rivier.' (If that is less than a day. Not far. Not near. That way. Down stream.) He points downstream.
The woman asks me for a cigarette. I give her four and she tucks one behind her ear and hands the other three to the man. She starts walking - upstream. After a moment the man follows her, hat in hand. All of us watch them as they walk away, until they become ghosts in the shimmer of the day and vanish from sight. Nobody says a thing. We walk without rest until after dark before we reach the pickup point. When we leave t' e river behind that evening, I don't look back. Years later I discover the rose quartz egg tucked inside a match box. I tip it into the palm of my hand and roll it around and place it in my mouth. I can taste

the river's age. The river is an eleven hour flight due south from where I'm standing with her stone in my mouth.

Perhaps a year-long walk - if you walk fast.

Or a lifetime - if you walk slow.

Friends Of Jesus: A postcard on the pavement outside my door. I pick it up and turn it over so I can see the image on the front. Beneath the spackle of pavement grime is a colour photograph of a scene I think I have seen before: a stream sprinkled with smooth stones, a monumental, almost architectural mountain dominating the background. The mountain glows like a tabernacle in the morning light. I don't know why I think it is dawn as opposed to dusk, but something in my marrow can feel the crisp morning air inside that canyon. It reeks of an African day. I can hear the trickle of water among the stones, birds twittering in the tall grass, smell the winter burnings on the breeze. I want it to be dawn.

Words printed below the image:

THE AMPHITHEATRE - DRAKENSBERG - SOUTH AFRICA

I flip the postcard over again. The message on the back is written in blue ballpoint. The letters are thick, sculpted, gouged into the surface of the cardboard as if the writer intended the message for a myopic reader:

LAST FEW DAYS IN
AFRICA, IN MOUNTAINS
-DRAKENSBERG RANGE.
AARON'S ANKLE NOT UP TO MUCH
HIKING BUT I HAVE
BEEN UP TO THE SUMMIT.
SOUTH AFRICA HAS
BEEN A REAL SURPRISE,
STUNNING LANDSCAPES
EVERYWHERE. OFF TO
VISIT AARONS PARENTS=
HOPE YOU ARE WELL
LOVE SARAH

In the top right hand corner, exactly where it should be, is a stamp. On the stamp is an image of a sleek whale in profile. I bring the postcard closer to my eyes to read the caption: SOUTHERN RIGHT WHALE Balaenidae eubalaena. I look at the address below the stamp. It is only a few doors down from where I'm standing. I consider delivering it just in case it somehow slipped unseen from the postman's hand when he removed a stack of mail from his bag. I pocket the postcard instead. I carry it with me wherever I go. I can't bring myself to discard it, part with it, surrender it to the darkness of the rightful letterbox. I believe the wind somehow carried it nine thousand miles from There to the spot outside my door over Here for me to find. I believe it must mean something. The postcard becomes a secret scrap of Home hidden about my person. I feel naked without it, lost. I go back for it every time I discover I've left it inside yesterday's jacket or shirt pocket. I fish it from its hiding place repeatedly, study the image on the front. Eventually I know every blade of grass, every water-worn boulder like I know the pockmarks on my face. The mountain lodges itself inside my mind. It grows larger, more solid. I commit the blue message to memory. It is a poem written specifically for me. I wonder who Sarah and Aaron are. I remember the names from Bible stories my mother used to read to me. I can't remember exactly who they were. Friends of Jesus? I carry the postcard around for a year before I finally Sellotape it to page twenty-nine in my diary. Fifty-three pages later in the same diary my father dies. I remember a holiday with my father and older brother thirty-five years ago somewhere near the postcard mountain.

White Chev Impala,
a borrowed caravan...
But those things are gone:
the Impala, the caravan.
My father, my brother.
The mountain is still there.
Exactly where we left it.
Solid.
Silent.
Unmoved.

Rough Blues for a Chev Impala

"Well the night's bursting open, these two lanes will take us anywhere..."
Thunder Road, Bruce Springsteen

She's the beast asleep on the back seat of my mind, she waits for the road, dreams of the streets, a haiku of chrome in small boy's dream. She's strong as an ox, white as a lie.

>And she waits for the streets, longs of the road.
>Her idle is a V8 sonnet written by Chevrolet.
>Her transmission is a poem hiding behind her grille.

Let's ride her again just for the hell of it, down to Giant's Castle, deep into the mountains, burn a white line through our dark land, just you and I while we still can.

>And she rumbles like thunder, purrs like a cat.
>She's a composition of engineering, a shimmering beast.
>She waits for the road, pines for the streets.

Open the old garage and let her out, let her free, drag her from her sleep. She's waiting in the past, lurking in the dark, dreaming of the road, praying for the streets.

>And I recall her body of cold chrome and steel.
>Her sleek lines smoother than the belly of an eel.
>She is stronger than an ox and whiter than a lie.

Let's take her out for one last trip, up into the mountains, down to the sea. I watch your hands, your hands on her wheel, as you steer her clear through the dark heart of our land.

>And she's perfectly clad in pure chrome and steel.
>Her lines are smoother than the belly of an eel.
>But she's heavier than an ox and bigger than a lie.

Let's take her out just for fun, for one last spin into the hub of my heart. I'll ride shot gun and you will drive - just us on that hard open road to the hollow heart of the past.

>And her lines are as soft as the murmurs of war.
>She's bigger and better than any myth.
>She's a white lie made of chrome and steel.

Her insides smell of sun-baked leather, she dreams of the road and longs of the streets. She's the time machine inside my dreams. She's the slumbering beast inside my head.

>And she's a myth made white by lies.
>She's the ox under the skin of an eel.
>She's a rusted memory of chrome and steel.

She's haunted me from the 60's through to now, a ghost machine with my dead father at the wheel. I keep her in the dark garage next to my crumbling boyhood house.

>She's a dream more slippery than the belly of an eel.
>She's a daydream bigger than an ox of chrome and steel.
>And she's a nightmare colder and wider than life itself.

Taste of Thoughts

Leaning from a window, arm straining into the storm,
I tried to catch rain in the palm of one hand.
You fetched a Chinese bowl from the kitchen,
said: *Here, it should be easier this way, more practical,*
rain is never caught by hand.

Then we sampled what little I caught,
rolled it around inside our mouths.
It tastes of metal, something old, you said.
I thought it's the taste of heaven silently rusting away,
final proof it's a shanty town, nothing up there is gold.

Storms bring unexpected thoughts.
You wouldn't have believed me about heaven anyway,
even if I'd said it out loud.
What do you think it tastes of, you asked.
Not much, I lied, *not much*, and licked the silent bowl.

A Sixteen Line Portrait of Fredrik in His Garden (Behind His Red House)

The first hot and nameless day of spring.
All afternoon he turns and tills the silent space,
snip-snips a decade's chaos from 14 apple trees,
furrows soil to lead astray the pending drought.

Now, six o'clock, slumped in a dog-tired chair,
he studies his slog, sips blister-black Hungarian wine.
To the south, he heard, locusts ate entire territories to the root,
elsewhere it rained frogs, fires laid waste to farms, gardens.

Somewhere behind him his wife's pitter-patter in the house,
the nameless child inside her still only the size of a peach stone...
Yet, the garden must be ready, ready for The Arrival. Fleckless...
This garden will be their child's first full view of the world.

Now, eight o'clock, a giddy-laughter of wild geese
wades through the thick orange-skin dusk to the sea.
Soon night will close in around him like an eyelid
and he'll sleep the sleep of conquerors inside his red house.

Seven for a Missing Friend

1.
Johnny Depp's Mouth:

The sun was behind you
when you shoved a photocopied flyer with Johnny Depp's mouth on it into my hand.
I am directing a play, your silhouette said,
a punk Western called *Cowboy Mouth*.

Within minutes we were talking dead crows, withdrawal symptoms and sea creatures
inside the humid confines of Café Petit Paris.
For the rest of the afternoon I bought the beers and you bummed one cigarette after another
off me.

We talked until the waiter stacked chairs on tables and mopped the floor around our feet.
I'd run out of cigarettes anyway so we left, kept the conversation flowing
as we moseyed through the city.

We had to lay foundations for a new faith.
We wanted to build a makeshift moon for us to live on.

You sounded like a station tannoy when you talked.
It would take me years of self-education
(mainly books you recommended by Auster, Nietzsche, Ondaatje, Kureishi, Hegel, Beckett,
etc. and your backcataloguememory of 70's American cinema)
to begin to pretend to understand you semi-properly.

On the final night of the play's run,
you roped me in to play the *Lobster Man*:
a taciturn Rock 'n' Roll hero trapped inside a home-made crustacean shell.
He emerges from the shell fully formed
- all silk shirt and leather pants and shades like a low-rent Bono –
and attempts suicide with an empty pistol in the full blaze of a spotlight.

Click!
Black Out.

2.
International Bastard:

You were an usher at a movie house somewhere in the States –
Milwaukee, I think it was.
It was when *Dog Day Afternoon* hit the world.
You told me how you watched *Dog Day Afternoon* six times a day, six days a week.
You became so obsessed with the dialogue you recorded the entire film on TDK C90 tapes
and listened to it over and over again.

I pictured you lying in your bed in the small hours
holding a squeaky tape recorder close to your ear
while a blizzard pounded the city
and a big-titted girl slept dreamlessly beside you.

(You always had a predilection for women with big tits:
...*her breasts tumbling like a waterfall towards my face...*)

I had never seen *Dog Day Afternoon* on account of The Cultural Boycott.
I'd heard of it, read about it, sat around smoking while you paced a variety of floors
recounting its narrative to me for the hundredth time:

Pacino: a confused, strung out homosexual in a straight world.
Poor John Cazale: brilliantly bewildered, doomed and jumpy as shit...

You had me in stitches every time,
you made them sound like some postmodern version of
Laurel & Hardy.

And I envied you.
I envied you your cultural adventures out in The World.
When I told you so you replied:
Do not envy me.
I am the International Bastard.
I'm always looking for a white stick in the Arctic.
I might never find one.

3.
Puke and Love in the Bathhouse

You said your mother saved your life and your mind
from Apartheid's rot when she packed you off to public school in England.
One afternoon, as we drove out of the city to explore
a hidden graveyard you'd discovered,
you told me two school stories that were like movie scenes.

Scene 1: According to you, your school had a pub each for staff and students. You were going through a rough patch (the details of which I now forget), and you went on a bender. You returned to your house pissed and hysterical and proceeded to puke in every single basin in the boy's room; the lower part of your face and hair caked with puke and bile. A shocked housemaster walked in on you and asked why you were puking in every available basin. You answered: *Because I am depressed*, and carried on puking.

Scene 2: You were in love with one of the boys in your school. The two of you met secretly in the bathhouse. You would run a bath and both of you would lie in the warm water holding each other. Not a whisper passed between you for fear of discovery. You would simply lie there listening to the dripping taps and breathing in steam and exhaling silence while your mates played Rugby on a muddy pitch on the other side of the wall.

I was almost in tears by the time we reached the graveyard.
Stories drizzled from your mouth like polished stones from a black pouch.

4.
Personal Hygiene Department

Your clothes were immigrants from better wardrobes.
You smuggled the odours of one season into the next inside the weave of your shirts,
navigated weeks and months in the same clothes you woke up in.

You found it amusing to tell people how you routinely went without a bath
or a change of clothes for several weeks or months at a time.
I commented on your ripeness countless times but you grinned and pleaded guilty.
Never judge a book by the smell of its pages, you seemed to say.

Hanging out with you in public places,
I prayed that nobody would think it was me
who was seriously lacking in the Personal Hygiene Department.
I have to give credit where credit's due:
You always inhabited your B.O. with élan.

5.
Maxim:

Never fear, you said one night in the grubby kitchen,
a jacket is always too big or too small even when it fits perfectly.

More than a decade later, I regularly test your maxim on men's outfitters.
You'll be happy to hear some of them agree with it.

As I sit here in this hollow room,
I imagine your words doing the rounds
at the annual International Convention of Men's Outfitters (ICMO?).
at the Marriott in downtown Tel Aviv or Acapulco.

From there your maxim spreads all over the world
and ends up being repeated to countless indecisive clients
in cut-price outlets
by salesmen
chasing incentives.

6.
20/20 Vision

You arrived late for our appointment and proudly showed off your new spectacle frames.
Found them, you said with a winner's smirk, *in an obscure optometrist's office,*
box after box containing a pandemonium of second hand frames
from behind the Iron Curtain.

I chose these, you said, *because they look like they could belong to some seventies*
Russian dissenter, or maybe to Pinter circa the Dumb Waiter years.
Point is, you added once the coffee arrived, *they cost next to nothing.*
Even the lenses are made of plastic. Here, tap them, see for yourself.
They are the Trabant of specs.
Like mobility, 20/20 vision shouldn't cost an arm and a leg.

You took a sip of coffee and your new specs fogged over like the windows
on the Trans Siberia Express.
When they cleared, you must have been surprised to see a vacant chair
where I had been sitting,
a half-smoked cigarette still smouldering in the ashtray,
beside it, some coins for the bill.
You probably nipped the cigarette and tucked the butt behind your ear for later.

You detested waste.

We never saw each other clearly after that.
Not really.

So much for bargain bin eyesight then.

Some time later I bumped into myself standing alone
on the darkened porch of a ramshackle farmhouse
inside a novel you wrote.
You had given me a new identity and a loaded shotgun.
I was squinting into a black and moonless night.